Smuggling
in The
Bristol Channel
1700 – 1850

GRAHAM SMITH

COUNTRYSIDE BOOKS

NEWBURY, BERKSHIRE

FIRST PUBLISHED 1989
© Graham Smith 1989

All rights reserved
No reproduction permitted
without the prior permission of the publishers:
Countryside Books
3 Catherine Road, Newbury, Berkshire

ISBN 1 85306 044 5

The cover illustration *Beach Landing*
is from a drawing by Edward Dowden

Produced through MRM Associates Ltd, Reading
Typeset by Acorn Bookwork, Salisbury
Printed in England by J.W. Arrowsmith Ltd, Bristol

Contents

Officer—Light Dragoons 1793

An Officer of Light Dragoons, one of the smugglers' most feared opponents.

Introduction

Smuggling . . . the very word has a ring of drama to it and is redolent of excitement, adventure, danger, daring, romance and intrigue. Over the years many writers and artists have perpetuated a very romantic view of smuggling. They have conjured up images of still moonlit coves, hidden caves, secret tunnels, lanterns flashing on lonely cliff-tops, lines of ponies trotting along dark and ancient paths laden with kegs of brandy, bales of tobacco and packages of tea and led by bands of jovial and swaggering characters dressed in gay and colourful clothes – almost as if they had just stepped out of a Gilbert & Sullivan operetta. By stark contrast the Revenue men, be they Customs or Excise, are invariably shown in dark and sombre clothing and depicted as taciturn, cold-hearted, cruel and, at times, cowardly – the natural opposition for the bold, handsome and fearless smuggler.

Thus the perfect scenario – good versus evil, right against wrong, the oppressed people battling against a faceless and callous authority. Many considered smuggling as the people's only answer to unjust laws. Laws that imposed penal and onerous duties on their few 'luxuries' in life – tea, gin and tobacco. Laws framed and passed by a distant Government in which they had no voice and whose burdens fell unfairly upon them in particular. Laws, which they felt, alienated their right to trade freely without the confines of high Customs duties and other import restrictions. Hence why those who were involved in the smuggling trade abhorred the use of the term 'smuggler' and proudly proclaimed themselves 'free-traders'. Smuggling, unlike most other illegal activities, was considered an honourable undertaking and even one to be proud of, because the only victim was the Government through lost revenues and after all the payment of taxes, in whatever form, has never been and never will be a popular pastime.

The smugglers or free-traders, as well as the majority of the public, did not consider that their activities were in any way wrong let alone criminal. The avoidance of harsh import duties was a laudable enterprise and all the more admirable if conducted with bravery and panache. As Charles Lamb wrote in the early 19th century, 'I like the smuggler, he is the only honest thief. He robs nothing but the Revenue, an abstraction I never greatly cared about.' Even Adam Smith, the famous economist, who was a high ranking Customs official in Scotland, felt some sympathy for the smuggler; he considered the laws of the country to be at fault rather

5

than the smuggler himself. An old boatman from Deal in Kent (a notorious smuggling place) recalling his younger days summed up a general attitude to the trade, 'Good days when a boatman might smuggle honest, didn't go a-stealing and wasn't afraid to die for his principles'. The majority of people through the Kingdom would say 'Amen' to that view.

So smuggling has passed into folklore clothed in a mantle of romance and respectability, a cosy and fairly harmless pursuit perpetrated by dashing and heroic characters for the good of the common people. Indeed what coastal town or maritime county does not proudly boast of their own intrepid smugglers, their guide books abound with 'typical smuggling bays', 'quaint old smuggling inns' and 'smugglers' lanes'. But however picturesque and attractive such romantic images of 'old-time' smuggling appear to us in the 20th century, such nostalgia must not be allowed to cloud the stark reality of the trade. These impressions are very, very far from the truth.

Smuggling was nothing more than a vicious, violent and bloody trade even when judged by the brutal standards of the time. Corruption, intimidation, terror, brutality, torture, treason and murder all played parts in the execution of the crime. The smuggling trade was conducted on a quite colossal scale and it extended throughout the country, penetrating deeply into every stratum of society. The evil influence and power of the smuggling fraternity has been likened to that of the Mafia, such was their vice-like control in many maritime areas. The smugglers were encouraged, supported and even financed by the local gentry. They were protected by compliant magistrates, condoned and pardoned by the clergy. At all times they were aided and abetted by the local people and had the sympathy and, at times, the support of the militia. In some areas they were even facilitated by venal revenue officers. At times of war they received active support from the enemy. Few paid the ultimate price for their crimes, most avoided transportation, service in the Royal Navy appeared to be the harshest penalty meted out to them. The goods they smuggled found their way into virtually all households in the land from the most lowly cottage to the highest estate.

The period from 1750 to 1830 has been rightly called the heyday of smuggling, at times the country was virtually besieged by smuggling gangs.

In 1781 Lord Pembroke asked, 'Will Washington take America, or the smugglers England first?'. He thought that the bet would be a fair and even one. Never before and never again would the country suffer such a prolonged state of lawlessness – the enormity and the violence of the smuggling trade surpassed any other form of illegal activity. At certain times, notably during the War of American Independence and the Napoleonic Wars, the authorities appeared to lose all semblance of control and there was a very real risk that the smugglers would take over many areas of the coast. Certainly most of the counties along the east and the south coasts were in a constant state of war with the smugglers. George Crabbe, the Suffolk poet, who lived through the height of the smuggling, wrote that the smugglers had gained 'a lawless passport through the land.'

Spare a thought for a moment for the poor and much maligned revenue officers of the times. It is against this backcloth of unbridled violence, terrorism and murder that their actions must be judged. They were always vastly outnumbered, universally despised and hated and they and their families lived as aliens in communities which whole-heartedly supported the smugglers. They received little or no help from the local population – the punishment meted out to informers was extreme – and were frequently obstructed in their duties. Often they had scant support from their superiors and the military. Their work was arduous, dangerous and poorly paid with little recompense for injuries sustained in the numerous smuggling affrays. It is therefore not surprising that many were none too energetic and vigilant in their endeavours. Some turned a blind eye to the seemingly insurmountable problem and a few found it easier and more profitable to be in the pay of the smugglers. Sad to relate though, even now, long after the dust of the battle has settled, the smugglers' past is cloaked in an unwarranted romantic aura, whereas the Customs men have died forgotten and no stone remains to record their passing.

Therefore to right some of those romantic myths. The brutality and violence used by the smugglers destroys any fond thought that they were 'gentlemen' – as is suggested in the famous Kipling poem. The smugglers normally avoided moonlit nights, preferring to work in the dark for quite obvious reasons. Furthermore, they usually waited for bad weather to arrange their smuggling runs, as on such nights there was less likelihood of the Revenue men and vessels being on patrol. Their greater knowledge of the local coast and, in the main, their superior seamanship enabled them to operate in the foulest of weathers. In fact in many areas, dark and stormy nights became known as 'smuggling weather'.

Again the use of caves and secret tunnels is somewhat of a myth. The smugglers generally preferred to move the goods in the open giving them a greater chance of escape. They also relied on superiority of numbers to ensure a successful landing, anything that reduced

7

this advantage – like a tunnel or narrow pathway, tended to be avoided. They also eschewed hiding places close to the shore – unless it was desperately necessary – they were well aware that the shores were regularly patrolled by riding officers and at times troops of dragoons. This was especially so after 1809 when the Preventive Waterguard kept a close watch on the near shore by using rowing galleys. The first essential after a successful landing was to transport the goods inland – if only for a mile or so. Most of the hiding places, according to Customs reports, were in the open country or in woods. These made the ultimate distribution of goods so much easier and safer. Churches and churchyards have gained a certain notoriety as smuggling hideaways and, indeed, there is much evidence to support this claim. However, it must be remembered that towards the end of the 18th century the smuggling trade had become so well organised that much of the smuggled cargo was delivered directly to individuals, who had pre-ordered it as if they were dealing with a local grocer.

As far as the colourful clothing was concerned, this appears to have been avoided at all costs as it made individuals easily identifiable. Customs reports from various areas of the coast seemed to agree that the smugglers wore a 'uniform' style of dress – a carter's smock with a vizard covering the lower part of their faces, and there are recorded instances of some men blacking their faces – all in an attempt to give them anonymity. It must be realised that the majority of men used to land and carry the smuggled goods were, in fact, farm labourers hired for the night and they had no alternative but to wear their working clothes.

It is my opinion that the reputation of so-called smuggling inns has been greatly overstated. Inns were regularly visited by Excise officers during their course of duty, not only to check stocks of spirits and wines but also to calculate the Excise duty on the beer brewed by the publican. No spirits or wine could be moved throughout the Kingdom unless they were covered by an official permit signed by an Excise officer to prove that they were duty-paid. The permit system had been introduced in the early decades of the 18th century in an attempt to control the movement of goods – in theory all spirits being conveyed without a permit were automatically considered smuggled. The same applied to goods found in a publican's stock. Therefore with the frequency of Excise visits the use of inns for the storage of smuggled goods was a very hazardous business indeed, especially as the officer had the legal right to search all parts of the premises, including the living quarters. Inns were more likely to have been used by smugglers as a rendezvous – a place where they could perhaps plan their next run without too much attention.

Stripped of some of the more romantic notions and much of the cant, the smuggling trade can be seen in its true light. There is no doubt that the subject has fascinated young and old alike for many, many years. The first smuggling myths started by word of mouth, then broadsheets, followed by popular songs such as *The Poor Smugglers Boy*, *The Smugglers Bridge*, *The Attack on Dover Gaol* and *Smuggler Bill*. It was not until the end of the 19th century that the first books on smuggling began to appear, perhaps the most famous being Falkner's *Moonfleet*. However, the true facts of the trade speak for themselves and need no author's embellishments; they provide a rich, dramatic and colourful story of an activity which for over 100 years almost reached the proportions of a national industry.

Graham Smith
1989

The 'Great Port' of Bristol – a view from Rownham Ferry c 1840.

S. Bradshaw

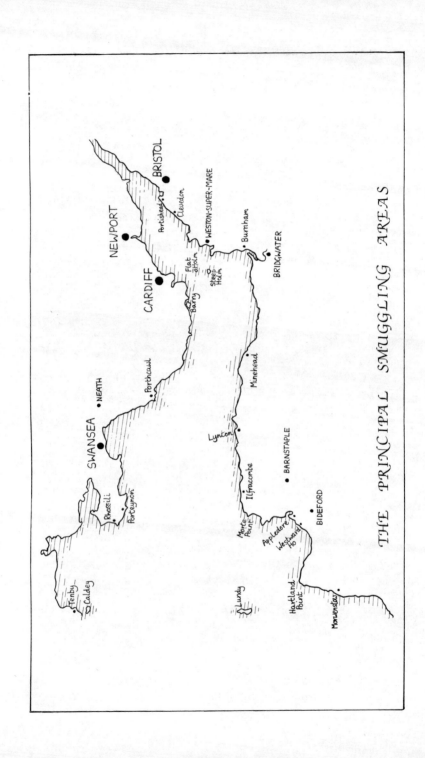

THE PRINCIPAL SMUGGLING AREAS

1
The Smuggling Trade

The origins of the trade can be traced back to the first organised imposition of Customs duties and the establishment of permanent Customs officials at the ports to collect those duties. The name itself is quite probably derived from a Low German word 'Smukkeln', which corresponds closely to 'smuckle' the earliest English word used. However, all the Scandinavian languages have similar words, 'Smugle' and 'Smuggla' – all mean virtually the same, 'hide', 'hiding hole'. The first recorded use of the word in English was in a Proclamation of 1661, 'A sort of lewd people called Smuckellors . . . who made it their trade to steal and defraud His Majesty of His Customs.'

The earliest references to smuggling or 'frauds' as the trade was then called are to be found in the late 13th century, largely as a result of the introduction, in 1275, of a new duty or 'custom' on exported wool. It is no coincidence that the Lord Chancellor sits on a woolsack, the wealth of England was founded on the excellence of its wool. This new high duty – it worked out to be the equivalent of about 40% by value – and the presence of a phalanx of collectors, comptrollers, surveyors and tronours (who weighed all goods to assess the duty payable) at the ports gave ample incentive to the merchants to avoid payment of duty on their shipments. Thus, unlike later smuggling, the early free-trade took the form of the illegal export of wool.

The honour, if one can call it so, of being the first recorded smuggler falls to Henry of Arderne, a wool merchant of some importance. Not only did he 'free-trade' in his own right but he also arranged shipments for other merchants. With the Exchequer spies close on his heels he escaped to Flanders, only to be caught in 1297 and brought to trial at the Exchequer Court, where he was fined heavily. His example was followed by many other merchants, who found that the seemingly insatiable Continental demand for English wool and the high export duties made wool smuggling a most profitable trade. It is of interest to note that Geoffrey Chaucer, a Customs Comptroller of wool in London Port, received in 1374, the

13

sum of £71 as his share in the proceeds of the sale of wool forfeited by a merchant for exporting it without duty. This seizure reward was a princely sum considering his annual salary only amounted to £16 13s 4d. Thus right from the outset can be seen the two essential features of the smuggling story. The presence of high duties to give the traders the incentive of large profits. And on the other side the presence of seizure rewards to give the Customs officers the incentive to seize smuggled goods in order to enhance their meagre incomes.

For the next 200 years or so the references to smuggling are rather spasmodic. There is no doubt that the trade continued but the extent of it is in doubt. There are several reasons to account for this situation. The major explanation was that for long periods the Custom duties were 'farmed'. By this system the King leased out the collection of duties at a port on an annual basis to financiers or merchants. In return the King and the Exchequer received an agreed sum quarterly, and by this method the revenue was obtained in advance without the expense of officers to collect it. Thus smuggling did not affect the Exchequer but rather harmed the Customs farmers' yield, hence the absence of reports of 'frauds on the Exchequer'.

Also for much of the period the Customs collectors were frequently prominent merchants in their own right. For instance Sir Richard Whittington was a customs Collector in London for several years. For such merchants the wearing of two hats obviated the need to smuggle. Furthermore there are many instances of collusion between the merchants and the Customs tronours. The Exchequer was forced to make many searching investigations into the various frauds at the ports.

During the 16th century large increases in all import duties created a climate where import smuggling also became an attractive proposition. However, the organisation of the Customs service had been greatly improved and also strict conditions were imposed on the control of vessels. The limits of each port were clearly defined, special legal quays were appointed for the loading and discharge of cargo and the hours of discharge were carefully regulated. Masters of vessels were compelled to report all their cargo at the Custom House before discharge was allowed and similarly for loading. Indeed this basis of Customs control of shipping is, with certain modifications, the system in operation today. The effect of these new regulations as far as smuggling was concerned was that any vessel found discharging or loading goods which were not reported and at a time or place not approved by the Customs, was considered to be smuggling *ipso facto*. An analogy may be made with today when a passenger goes through the green channel with extra dutiable goods. Part and parcel of the wave of new efficiency was the greater supervision of Customs staff and the encouragement to exert their authority. The effect of this increased vigilance can be seen in a riot at Lyme Regis in 1576; most of the vessels there were suspected of smuggling and the actions of a keen new officer caused a tumult and only the intervention of the Mayor prevented bloodshed. There were troubles in other parts of the country as Collectors attempted to enforce some semblance of control. Although one Collector reported in 1596 that so much was wrong with his port that even if he had 500 men, which of course he did not, he could not hope to bring about any reforms. As long as recognised trade brought the Exchequer a reasonable revenue the task of tackling the smuggling problem was left to another day.

Considering its subsequent importance in the smuggling trade, tobacco was at first lightly taxed following its introduction into the country in the 1560s. It was James I who called it 'the pernicious weed, the very abomination of the Devil' and tried to tax it out of existence. He raised the duty from 2d per lb to 6s 8d per lb, which clearly placed it out of the reach of the general public and overnight created a powerful stimulant for smuggling. Though the high duty was reduced later, restrictions were placed on its import and successive Governments found it a most useful item to tax, so much so that tobacco remained the most smuggled commodity for well over 300 years.

However, the illegal export of wool or 'owling' was still the most pressing problem. The term 'owling' and 'owlers' for the wool smugglers is said to be derived from their propensity to work at night, although another source has suggested that the word is a corruption of 'woolers'. Except for certain isolated instances the owling trade was concentrated on the Sussex, Kent and Essex coasts, with the Romney Marsh being the most notorious area. During 1669 the House of Lords debated the vexed question and some Customs officers came up from Dover to give their views. They reported that the number of owlers had greatly increased and that they now operated in large well-armed gangs. It was suggested that troops be stationed in every village along the coast to keep a constant watch and patrol. An ominous sign for the future was the number of 'fights and affrays between the owlers and the Revenue men'. Unfortunately nothing tangible resulted from the inquiry – shelving the problem once again.

The last decade of the 17th century saw a quite dramatic increase in smuggling, which can be largely attributed to two main factors. 15

Perhaps the most significant was the introduction and rapid development of the fore and aft rigging, which completely revolutionised sailing techniques, certainly as far as coastal waters were concerned. The dangers of strong tides, rock shallows and the nearness to the shore made the ability to sail to windward and to tack of vital importance. Thus the technical advantages of the new rig had a profound effect on the growth and development of smuggling.

Previously square rigged vessels could only enter creeks on a favourable wind and would have to remain there until the wind was in the right quarter to make their escape – hence their chance of discovery was quite great. The small fore and aft vessels could now sail into any creek or inlet, load or unload their illegal cargo and leave irrespective of the direction of the wind. It was Charles II who had introduced yachts into the country and soon vessels based on a yacht design were being constructed specially for the smuggling trade; their main features were speed, lightness of construction, cheapness, manoeuvrability and shallow draft to enable them to operate close to the shore. With such vessels the English Channel had been reduced to a very narrow stretch of water.

This technical breakthrough came at an apt time just when there was a vast increase of import duties of all kinds as well as the introduction of various trade restrictions and prohibitions. These increases were largely as a result of 'The Glorious Revolution' of 1688, by which the country was drawn into war with France and forced to maintain a large and expensive army in Ireland to prevent invasion by James II. Such policies required a large revenue, hence the duty increases. Quite naturally these swingeing increases gave rise to a smuggling boom – tobacco, silks, lace, spices and brandy were now increasingly smuggled. The greater the success of the smugglers the less the revenue yield, which resulted in further increases to make up the shortfall, which in turn only fuelled the smugglers' efforts – a vicious circle and one to be replicated frequently over the next hundred years.

It was during these years that the Excise officers first entered the smuggling fray. The first Excise duty had been introduced in 1643 and was imposed on home-produced goods, such as beer and ale, spirits, salt and leather. The Excise service was completely separate from the Customs service and remained so until 1909 when the two services amalgamated to form the modern Customs and Excise department. As part of the 'taxation package' an Excise duty (in addition to the Customs duty) was placed on imported brandy. So for the first time Excise officers became concerned with smuggled

THE EXCISEMAN OUTWITTED.

A Countryman was stopped by a Revenue Officer at Burlesdon, where he took two Casks of Spirits, which he supposed to be smuggled. After the Officer had carried the Liquor from Burlesdon to Titchfield, a Distance of three Miles, the Man suddenly stopped at a House, saying, "It is to be left there." The Officer replied, 'No, as I have seized it, it must go to the Excise Office,' and immediately proceeded with the Casks. 'Not so fast, Master,' replied the Countryman, 'I have a little bit of Paper here, which if you will take the Trouble of reading, you will find it to be left at this House.' The Officer having read the Paper, exclaimed, 'Why, you Rascal! this is a Permit, why did'nt you shew it me before.' 'Because,' said he, 'if I had, you would not have been so kind to have carried the Liquor so far for me.'

Printed and Sold by R. HARRILD, 20, Great Eastcheap.

Excise Permits were a fundamental part of the control of duty-paid goods.

17

goods. They had, in fact, a small vessel stationed at Deal 'to prevent the running of brandies on the coast and to other ships lying in the Downs.'

However, it was still the illegal export of wool that caused the greatest problem. On parts of the Kent and Sussex coasts it was thought that 'every house was an owlers'. A contemporary report described the owlers as, 'a militia that in defiance of all authority, convey their wool to shallops with such strength that the officers dare not offend them.' The situation was so grave that in 1690 the Customs Board decided to establish eight 'riding officers' for the first time. These officers, so beloved by certain romantic novelists, were based at the notorious owling towns of Lydd, Hythe, Romney and Folkestone. Each was allocated a stretch of coast to patrol day and night. The new force did not improve matters, on the contrary the situation worsened. The officers were ridiculously outnumbered and at sea the heavily armed French privateers had little or no opposition. In 1696 the Admiralty were enjoined to provide armed vessels to cruise from the North Foreland to the Isle of Wight and 'to seize any ships that export wool'. This was the first instance of official co-operation between the Navy, and the Customs in the prevention of smuggling.

In spite of these new measures the position further deteriorated and was rapidly getting out of hand. It was estimated that over 120,000 packs of wool were being smuggled. In 1699 a new 'Landguard' comprising over 50 riding officers was introduced to cover the coast from the Isle of Sheppey to Chichester. These officers received £90 per annum, to include the cost of a servant and a horse. As well as the new Landguard, Customs sloops were stationed at ports from Weymouth round to Whitehaven and from Newcastle down to Wivenhoe. This was really the birth of the Revenue fleet, which for many decades was second in size only to the Royal Navy. The first Customs vessel had come into service over 30 years earlier and its first seizure at sea had been a cargo of 'drugges and quicksilver'. Obviously not the sort of drugs that the present-day cutter service are involved with. It was also decided to strengthen the coastal patrol all along the south and west coast as far as Padstow. Officers were even stationed along the border with Scotland 'to prevent the clandestine trade'. Smuggling had come of age, it was now a nationwide problem.

Thus at the beginning of the new century the lines of battle had been drawn up for the desperate struggle that lay ahead. On the land there were the riding officers and the Excise officers, aided at times by the military, and at sea the Customs and Excise vessels, helped rather infrequently by the Navy. For the next 130 years these forces would be at almost constant war with the smugglers, with varying success.

In less than a lifetime, the face and extent of smuggling had drastically changed. The trade blazed throughout the country like a forest fire, no part was immune from its evil grip. Though the south coast right from the Thames Estuary to Lands End was the most notorious area, obviously from its close proximity to the Continent, the West Country and Wales were quite adequately supplied by bands of smugglers based in Ireland. The North West and Scottish coasts were served by the Isle of Man, which was 'a nest of smugglers, who glory in their treasons, the whole island lives on smuggling' (indeed the same could be said of the Channel Isles). The East Coast smugglers naturally looked to the Low Countries to supply their wants.

It was not just the coastal areas that were affected by the trade, it penetrated far inland. In 1705 a force of 'land carriage men' were appointed in London. No less than 17 were required for the capital and their specific duties were to watch the coaching inns and to examine the various carriages on arrival to ensure that no smuggled goods had been carried from the ports. They also had powers to search the inns and warehouses. Certainly they were quite successful with seizures of silks, lace, bullion and toilet waters – the top end of the market! Later they were established in Bristol, Newcastle and Norwich. Hounslow Heath, Clapham Common and Epping Forest were used as supply depots for smuggled goods. Smuggled tea even found its way into the Fleet prison! Out in the country the hawkers, the packmen and the drovers were the means by which smuggled goods found their way into virtually every village and hamlet throughout the Kingdom. The number of recorded seizures by Excise officers miles inland suggests that the stories of the famous Wiltshire 'moonrakers' could really apply to any inland county.

As the Customs – and to a lesser extent the Excise – struggled manfully to contain the trade, Parliament continually brought out new legislation or reframed existing Acts in an attempt to combat it. Each successive Act became more drastic, the penalties harsher, with the result that the legislation became self-defeating. In 1718 it was enacted that any vessel of 50 tons or under, laden with tea, brandy or French silks found 'hovering' within two leagues (six miles) of the coast was liable to seizure – the first of many 'Hovering Acts' that were passed during the century. Three years later it was enacted that any boat of more than four oars found on the coast 19 would be forfeited and destroyed by 'cutting in three'. Receivers of smuggled goods were liable to three months imprisonment and convicted smugglers to seven years transportation. However, despite all this legislation the main difficulty was in getting a conviction, generally the magistrates sided with the smugglers and as for the jury cases they were almost totally in favour of the smuggling fraternity – after all they and their families had to live and work in the community. The perversion of justice was so blatant that often Revenue officers found themselves on trial for assault though in truth they were only defending themselves from brutal attacks at the hands of gangs of smugglers, who vastly outnumbered them.

The first of many Parliamentary Inquiries into the smuggling trade sat in 1736 under the chairmanship of Sir John Cope. Its report conveyed to Parliament (possibly for the first time in such strong terms) the incredible trade:

'The smugglers being grown to such a degree of insolence, as to carry on their wicked practices by force and violence, not only in the country and the remote parts of the Kingdom, but even in the City of London itself, going in gangs armed with swords, pistols and other weapons, even to the number of forty or fifty, by which means they have been too strong, not only for the officers of the Revenue but for the civil magistrates themselves ... The number of Custom House officers who have been beaten abused and wounded since Christmas 1723 being no less than 250, besides six others who have been actually murdered in the execution of their duty.'

The report resulted in even sterner legislation, which brought in the death penalty for hindering or wounding Revenue officers. The Act did, however, offer a free pardon for past smuggling offences, providing full details were disclosed and associates named. A not very successful idea as few smugglers were prepared 'to grass' as the retribution meted out to informers was normally death. As the legislation became more draconian it did little to combat the extent of the trade, in fact it actually exacerbated the situation as the smugglers used far greater violence to ensure that they were not taken, as capture automatically meant the death penalty.

For sheer brutality the gangs operating in Kent and Sussex were quite unsurpassed in the whole history of smuggling. Towns such as Lydd, Hastings, Deal, Dover, Folkestone and Rye were virtually in the complete control of these gangs. The Groombridge, the Mayfield, the Ruxley and the Hawkhurst gangs have all passed into smuggling folklore. They worked both by day and night, often over 100 strong and moved like small armies terrorising the whole countryside. They were quite prepared to do pitched battle with the

Revenue and military alike. They maimed and killed with a callous impunity. Nothing seemed too outrageous or dangerous for them to tackle. They attacked gaols to release their comrades and broke into Custom Houses to retrieve their seized goods. They kidnapped Customs officers and transported them over to France where they were imprisoned until the Customs Board could bargain for their release. Though other smuggling gangs operating in other parts of the country were equally successful – for instance the Hadleigh gang in Suffolk, Gulliver's band in Dorset, the Beer gang of Devon, the Carter family in Cornwall, Knight and Connor in the Bristol Channel, Yawkins in the north-west and the Browning family in the north-east – the utter brutality and quite mindless violence was missing. There has never been an adequate explanation why Kent and Sussex should produce such savage smugglers.

At sea the situation was equally desperate. By 1750 the vessels used in the smuggling were so large, well-armed and commanded with such verve that they easily repulsed any attacks from the Revenue vessels. As one Customs commander reported, 'we are actually in danger of being run down and sunke by them, who have not only threatened to do so but also attempted it.' Some Revenue vessels were actually destroyed by the smugglers, a few were captured, the crew set adrift and the vessels then used in the smuggling trade. The smugglers were not even intimidated when opposed by Naval vessels, they treated them in the same insolent manner. In fact the Royal Navy made little or no impact on the war against smuggling until the end of the French wars. Indeed there were many instances of Naval officers and seamen being caught smuggling. Relations between the Navy and the Customs were never very cordial.

It is virtually impossible – due to the nature of the trade – to try to quantify the amount and value of goods smuggled and the disastrous effect on the country's trade and revenue. Although Customs collectors were often called upon to give estimates of smuggling in their ports, they were quite understandably reluctant to admit to large scale smuggling in their areas as such reports would be tantamount to admitting a laxity and inefficiency of control on their part or, perhaps even worse, collusion. Therefore all figures of smuggled goods are likely to be under-estimated and furthermore statistics of seized goods can be somewhat misleading and are unreliable as a guide to the totals of smuggled goods.

In 1729 the Yarmouth collector reckoned that 49,000 half-ankers of brandy (roughly equivalent to 180,000 gallons) were landed each year on the East coast. And some four years later the Treasury

21

The London Custom House in the 18th century, where the Customs Board sat.

calculated that in one year 54,000 lbs of tea and 123,000 gallons of brandy had been seized in Kent and Sussex alone, and they considered that this was less than one fifth of the total smuggled. It is safe to say that at least £3 millions of goods were being smuggled annually at a time when the total legal trade of the country was about £11 to £12 millions, thus the country was losing at least one quarter of its revenue and quite probably the figure was even higher.

For a large part of the 18th century the staple commodity of the smuggler was tea (or 'dry goods' as they called it). Legal tea was relatively expensive, the East India Company had a monopoly of import and all tea legally sold in the country passed through its tea auctions in the City of London. Thus the combination of a trade monopoly and high duties – both Customs and Excise – made tea smuggling very profitable. It was also almost a perfect commodity to smuggle, easily obtainable on the Continent or from East Indiamen, light to transport and with a high value in proportion to its bulk.

Much of the smuggled tea was bought in Holland for as little as 6d to 1s per lb depending on quality. This tea could be sold for anything from 4s up to 10s per lb. The cheapest legal tea in London cost about 5s per lb and elsewhere nearly 50% more. Parson Woodforde of Norfolk obligingly left a diary and an entry for March, 1777 records him paying 'Andrews the smuggler' 10s 6d per lb. Such were the profits to be made in tea smuggling and they could be made even greater by the judicious use of dyed leaves to adulterate the tea, which was quite a common practice. By 1750 it was estimated that 3 million lbs were smuggled annually, more than three times the legal trade and 20 years later the figure was thought to have risen to over 7 million lbs.

In 1784 one of William Pitt's first steps on becoming Prime Minister was to reduce the duty from an equivalent 125% duty right down to 12½%. With this one stroke he made tea smuggling virtually unprofitable. The success of the change could be seen in the very first year when the legal sales increased almost threefold. Although the tea duty was increased in later years tea smuggling became relatively non-existent – a good example of how to counter the smuggling problem. Perhaps one good thing came out of tea smuggling. At the beginning of the 18th century tea was a fashionable but expensive luxury enjoyed by comparatively few, but by the end of the century it was in common use even in the households of the very poor – a nation of tea-drinkers had been born!

With tea no longer worth carrying the smugglers increased their trade in other goods – tobacco, brandy and geneva – and during the French wars at the end of the century, anything that was French, as those goods were completely prohibited. Silks, lace, kerchiefs, gloves and even glassware were all at a premium so the smugglers could almost name their price as there were no legal goods as a comparison. Tobacco could be purchased for as little as 3d per lb and sold in the country for 1s 3d to 1s 6d per lb. Quite a lot of the tobacco had been imported legally with the duty paid. On exportation the duty was refunded – only for this same tobacco to find its way back into the country in a matter of a week or so as smuggled! French brandy could be bought for as little as 1s 6d to 2s 6d per gallon and Parson Woodforde records that in 1800 he paid 'his smuggler' 21s for a gallon.

Geneva has an interesting social history. The word is derived from the French 'genevre' = juniper. The spirit, which was Dutch in origin, was first introduced into the country by William III. The first sales of gin were slow but soon English distillers found how cheap it was to produce. Within a short time the sales of gin far exceeded that of beer and ale. The spirit could be bought almost everywhere, even from street barrows and carts. The sign 'Drunk for 1d, Dead Drunk for 2d, Straw for nothing' appeared in the windows of shops and inns. The straw was for sleeping off the effects of the spirit! Gin had become the drink of the working classes. There was so much drinking that it was a grave social problem, and Hogarth's print *Gin Lane* was no exaggeration. Excise duties were increased and penal licence fees put legitimate producers out of business and 23 opened the door for illicit distillers and, of course, the smugglers. Geneva or gin or Hollands was cheap to produce and could be purchased for as little as 9d to 1s per gallon and sold for 4s to 6s a gallon. By the end of the century it had once again achieved respectability as a 'middle class' drink, largely as a result of smuggling.

The whole of the smuggling trade was very profitable for everyone from the financial backer right down to the merest labourer. Indeed it could even be so for 'the opposition', the seizure rewards for Revenue officers could be quite sizeable. Though having said that there were very few Revenue officers who managed to retire in comfort on the proceeds of seized goods.

Although in the early years of the century smuggling was largely conducted on an 'ad hoc' basis, and comprised fishermen turning to the trade to eke out a poor season, but as soon as it was realised that the trade was hugely profitable, smuggling became highly organised as befits a large and thriving industry.

The merchants who financed the purchase of the smuggled goods were frequently long established and outwardly respectable traders in the community. In many cases members of the local gentry were quite prepared to back the smugglers. Quite often the Customs had very strong suspicions about these shadowy 'godfathers' but had no evidence, nor indeed were they ever likely to get any, to proceed against them. The backers almost invariably acted through an agent, who dealt directly with the master smuggler, agreeing the percentage profits and what goods his principal and his friends required. The backers viewed the financing of smuggling as no different to any other 'venture' investment, except of course that it was far more profitable. It was estimated that by the 1770s over £1 million in coin was exported each year to pay for the smuggled goods. Though in 1770 William Hickey, whilst on return from India, was on board an East India vessel in the Channel when he witnessed a smuggler take delivery of a variety of goods and calmly pay by means of a cheque for £1,200 drawn on a London bank. According to the Captain of the East Indiaman, 'These people [the smugglers] always deal with the strictest honour . . .' Certainly after the Napoleonic Wars much of the payment for smuggled goods was arranged by bankers' drafts – just the same as the legal trade.

The shipmaster, who arranged the purchase and brought over the goods in his vessel,was paid handsomely for what was a small risk; at least in the early days when there were few Revenue vessels and most of the seizures were made on land. However, he was vitally important to the success of the operation. Firstly for his contacts in the French ports which enabled him to purchase at competitive prices and, more importantly, for his expertise as a 'spotsman'. His innate navigational skills and intimate knowledge of the local coast meant that he could bring his vessel as close as possible to the pre-arranged spot, where the landers were waiting – hence the name. Often the runs were completed in bad weather and poor visibility, and the master would only have the odd faint light to guide him so his knowledge of the coast and his seamanship were vital; a mis-judgement of a mere hundred yards or so could jeopardize the whole operation and nullify all the careful and elaborate preparations made on shore.

The largest share of the profits was taken by the master smuggler on land. It was he who arranged the unloading, dispatch, storage and the ultimate disposal of the goods. He took the greatest risks but the profits were so huge that it was suggested that he could afford to lose two cargoes out of three and still make a handsome profit. As the Revenue forces were never this successful – the ratio was more likely one in ten or even more – the smuggling master could with careful planning, good organisation and a little luck become very rich. For instance Arthur Gray of the Hawkhurst gang was reputed to be worth over £50,000 with a large mansion to boot. And Isaac Gulliver retired to a country estate near Wimborne in Dorset.

The logistical problems in managing a successful landing were formidable and needed a person of exceptional organisational flair, as well as leadership qualities – motivation by fear was not the real answer. Getting sufficient landers, animals and carts to a given spot, planning the various routes to be taken, pre-arranging storage bases and subsequent delivery to the customers were large tasks, espe-cially as they were undertaken in darkness, on rough and inferior paths and tracks and with the constant threat of a Revenue ambush. Though the prime motivation was money, there is no doubt much truth to the view expressed by Dostoyosky that a smuggler, 'works from inclination. He is on one side an artist. He risks everything, runs terrible risks and gets out of scrapes, and sometimes acts with a sort of inspiration. It is a passion as strong as gambling.'

So much for the main principals in the affair. The supporting cast in this grand performance – the landers, the tubmen, the look-out men and the batmen – were normally recruited, on a nightly basis, from the labouring poor of the port and locality and were, more often than not, farm workers. Generally they would receive 10–12s for a few hours work as well as a free dollop of tea and maybe some geneva. This compared very favourably with the average weekly wage for a farm hand of 8–10s. Farmers close to the coast had considerable trouble to find enough workers especially at harvest time. The smuggling master demanded utmost loyalty and a conspiracy of silence if they were unlucky enough to be caught, although in fairness their family were usually looked after should they be gaoled.

The tubmen had the most physically demanding job of all. They were employed as 'human packhorses', to carry two half-ankers of spirit slung over their shoulders. Thomas Hardy tells of an old tubman in Dorset who remembered, 'the horribly suffocating sensation produced by a pair of spirit tubs slung upon the chest and back after stumbling with the burden of them for several miles inland over rough country and in darkness.' These poor men, the real drudges of the trade, ran a far greater risk of capture by the Revenue. There are many recorded instances of them spending months upon months in gaol for debt, as the Customs had the legal right to impose compromise penalties for minor smuggling offences. During the French wars many of them were pressed either into the Navy or the Army.

As for the batmen, as their name implies they carried 'bats'. These were stout wooden staves, often iron-tipped and at least six feet long, to enable them to ward off the swords and cutlasses of the Revenue men as well as being a very effective weapon, especially to unseat men on horseback. The batmen were, in essence, the security guards who were there to protect the valuable cargo and assist the nucleus of regular gang members, who always rode well-armed with pistols, swords and loaded whips.

To complete the picture, the smugglers received almost universal support from the rest of the community. Farmers willingly left stables and barns unlocked to allow the smugglers to 'borrow' their animals and carts. Packages of tea and gin were left when their property was returned. The women often took an active role in proceedings. It was suspected but not proven that the smugglers' wives in Beer had attacked a riding officer and thrown him to his death from a cliff-top. They were frequently employed to make fires on the cliffs to act as signals or warnings and many wives were used to deliver the goods. Though the highly romanticised 19th century novel of a woman smuggler of Suffolk called *Margaret Catchpole* was supposed to have been based on true facts, no evidence has been found to support the story.

Most of the smuggled goods originated in the ports across the Channel. Flushing and Ostend both had flourishing communities of English smugglers, who had taken refuge there. Much of the geneva or 'Hollands' which was smuggled came from Schiedam, where by 1780 the several distilleries were producing in excess of four million gallons a year. And at Ostend several tobacco manufacturers supplied tobacco in convenient sizes and in special waterproofed packages solely for the trade. Dunkirk also had several distilleries occupied fully in providing spirits for the smugglers. During the wars Napoleon allotted a large part of the town to English smugglers, such did he consider their importance to the French economy.

Further west Dieppe, Cherbourg and Le Havre relied almost completely on the smuggling trade. The port of Nantes was one of the first French ports to appreciate the value of the English free-traders, especially as far as brandy was concerned. In fact in the trade French brandy was known as 'Nantz'. Indeed there is an instance, in 1792, of Robert Burns, the poet and Exciseman, sending his patroness Mrs Dunlop, 'a very small jar, sealed full of as genuine Nantz as ever I tasted.' Dumfries is a long, long way from Nantes – such were the tentacles of the trade!

The Channel Islands were for many years a rich and abundant source of goods, so much so that they were called the 'den of smugglers', where everybody seemed to be actively engaged in the trade. And although English Customs officers were stationed on both Jersey and Guernsey in 1767, it was many years before the smugglers were finally forced away. They immediately moved to neighbouring ports on the Brittany coast, such as St Malo and Roscoff. Within a short space of time both ports flourished, with special warehouses being built to accommodate the illegal trade. Both Jersey and Guernsey still continued their profitable industry – the manufacture of small kegs for smuggled spirits.

The Isle of Man, as already mentioned, was the centre of smug-gling activities in the Irish Sea and when the Government purchased the island in 1765 and established a Customs force there, the trade merely moved to Ireland. Rush, which had hitherto been a small and quiet fishing port just north of Dublin, suddenly blossomed as the entrepot for smuggled goods destined for Wales, the West Country, the North West and Scotland.

From its inception in the previous century the East India Com-pany vessels were a thorn in the flesh of the Customs. The officers and crew were always active in selling tea, silks and spices to smuggling vessels who met them on their way up the Channel. So bad was the problem that Revenue vessels would escort them from the Downs right to their berth in London port. However, this was like shutting the stable door after the horse had bolted, as most of the goods had already been traded further down the Channel and outside the six mile limit where the Customs vessels were powerless to interfere. And further west the West Indian vessels trading to Plymouth, Bristol, Liverpool and Whitehaven were met by the smugglers in the western approaches and they proved to be valuable sources of rum, sugar and tobacco.

By the middle of the century considerable quantities of smuggled   27 goods found their way into the country carried by passengers via the various packet ports. Harwich was a notorious port – in 1790 a commander of an Excise cutter actually had the effrontery to seize one of the regular packet boats because so many smuggled goods were found concealed on board. The enraged reaction to this unique incident produced accusations of 'unfair practice' by the Excise and after appeal to the Treasury the vessel was released – only to continue smuggling time and time again. Dover was one of the foremost smuggling posts, which comes as no great surprise. It was used continually by members of the Diplomatic service, Government messengers and other quasi-Government figures and it was the fond belief of the Customs Board (probably fully justified) that goods were smuggled under the cover of the diplomatic bags and in boxes secured by consular seals. The Customs had no legal right to open such packages. But it was at Falmouth where smuggling was rife. The passengers and crews of the postal packets brought in an estimated £3 millions of goods annually, of which the majority were smuggled. This trade was considered 'the best support of the town – it was a veritable storehouse of merchandise.'

In 1780 the Government took a quite unprecedented step when it issued a pamphlet entitled *Advice to the Unwary*, which attempted to

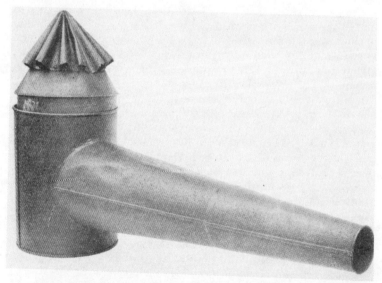

A spout lantern. Held in the crook of the left arm, the signaller's right hand covered the end of the spout, and then was removed to show a pin-point flash of light to the incoming lugger.

explain and justify the extreme severity of the smuggling legislation
It also tried to bring home to the public at large the extent of
smuggling. The legislation was needed as a result of, 'the gangs of
daring and dissolute persons armed with offensive weapons.' The
pamphlet maintained that the trade pervaded every city, town,
village and hamlet bringing universal distress to the fair trader;
3,870,000 gallons of geneva were thought to be smuggled annually
as well as five to six million lbs of tea, the lost revenue to the country
on these two items alone was thought to be in excess of £3 million
each year. In order to get some concept in modern terms one could
multiply the figure by 100 and perhaps even more – it makes today's
estimates of the 'black economy' pale into insignificance!

Five years later, after yet another smuggling inquiry, it was
thought that smuggling had even increased threefold. The smugglers were reported to be carrying on, 'a system of business, which
set all the laws of the country at defiance'. The situation was so grave
that large areas of the country were in a state of virtual anarchy –
desperate problems required desperate remedies. And William Pitt
the Younger seemed to be just the man for the task. We have already
seen the effect of his reduction in the tea duty and now he seemed
prepared to take the battle to the smugglers. In January 1785 he
initiated action, which really heralded the next phase in the war
against smuggling. On being informed that due to the severity of the
winter most of the smuggling boats in Deal were laid up on the
beach, Pitt ordered a large detachment of troops to march on Deal
and destroy as many vessels as possible. The troops encountered
only token resistance from the inhabitants, who were forced to watch
helplessly as all the vessels were fired. This was the first example of a
positive act of retaliation against any smugglers and it signalled a
new determination to tackle the seemingly insurmountable problem.

By now the most important and most successful means for the
suppression of smuggling were the Revenue vessels. They numbered
45 and operated from Newcastle right round the coast to Whitehaven,
as well as in Scotland and Ireland. Most were clinker-built (with
lapped planking) of a very sturdy construction and with a great sail
area for their size. The main feature of these vessels was the
bowsprit, which was almost two thirds the size of the hull to give the
vessels extra speed. Some of the cutters built after the turn of the
century were the fastest vessels afloat. Armed with the new carro-
nade guns or 'smashers' they were beginning to compete with the
smuggling vessels on almost equal terms. For the next 50 years they
took the war to the smugglers and the majority of large seizures of
smuggled goods were made by the Revenue vessels. Contemporary
prints and engravings have left us with vivid and dramatic pictures

29

of these cutters in full sail ploughing through the water, pennants flying and guns blazing as they went in hot pursuit of their quarry. Splendid images of the days of 'old time' smuggling and the romantic days of sail.

With the advent of the long and bitter war with France in 1793, all hopes of a reduction of duties disappeared. All Customs and Excise duties increased and new ones were introduced – income tax reared its ugly head for the first time. As the war dragged on and on so the duties increased to fund the enormous cost of waging war on land and at sea. For instance by 1815 tobacco duty had risen to 3s per lb – almost three times the amount at the advent, and tea duty mounted steadily throughout the war years until it reached 96%. All trade with France was strictly prohibited, though French brandy was still being drunk by the upper classes of society and indeed by members of the Government without any apparent conscience! With many of the Revenue vessels seconded to fleet duties and few dragoons left to assist the Revenue, the coastline was left to a handful of riding officers and the odd preventive boat as the only defence. High duties, near-siege conditions and a depleted Revenue service were ideal conditions for a fresh impetus to smuggling.

The French government actively encouraged smuggling. Despite the war English smugglers were given free access to the French Channel ports. The French urgently required English gold coins; it is doubtful whether they could have paid their armies without the steady influx of English gold. It was estimated that about £10,000 in coin was being smuggled out of the country each week. Long rowing galleys specially for the trade were built in France, they became universally known as 'guinea boats'. Rowed by up to twelve men they were fairly fast – by repute up to nine knots – very difficult to sight especially in the dark and, not being controlled by the wind, they could take quick evasive action. The success of these galleys can be gauged by the very few that were seized. The trade died a natural death after the peace treaty of 1814. However, one can only admire the seamanship and courage of the guinea smugglers who were prepared to row up to 30 or so miles in the treacherous Channel waters in all weathers.

Equally important to the French was the information about defences and the movement of vessels that the smugglers brought with them. Many of the smugglers saw the sale of such information as an added bonus, like many intellectuals in the country they were in favour of the French Revolution. The 'letters for a spy' carried by Kipling's smugglers was not very far from the truth. Napoleon commented, during his exile, on the smugglers' activities. He claimed,

' . . all the intelligence I received from England came through the smugglers. They are likeable people and have courage and ability to do anything for money. They brought over newspapers and despatches from the spies we had in London, landed them and hid them in their houses. They are genti terribili.'

Equally it must be said that many smugglers served with distinction in the Navy as pilots. Certainly nobody could question that they were very fine seamen, the Navy were always delighted to take smugglers as pressed men.

Along the south coast a system of 'Sea Fencibles' had been established; these were basically licensed fishing boats, whose crews were issued with arms especially to guard against the likely invasion. They formed a kind of floating Home Guard but unfortunately for the Revenue they were, according to the Customs Collector at Cowes, 'all in the smuggling trade and consider that they have now been given a licence to conduct their illegal trade.' An added problem and concern was the standard and efficiency of the riding officers. Many were well over the age of 50 years and thus quite unsuited for what was a physically demanding job, patrolling in all weathers in difficult and dangerous conditions, as well as a frustrating one, as they always appeared to be one, if not, two steps behind the smugglers. It was also maintained that many only rode out on 'their own private business', the majority fabricated their journals and some were thought to be acting as agents for the smugglers. One officer in Kent was graphically described as 'being no more use than a gull on the beach'! These opinions and misgivings were expressed by a member of the Customs Board, who deliberated from the warmth, safety and comfort of the London Custom House – a far, far cry from the cold, inhospitable and dangerous clifftop on a dark winter's night!

In an attempt to strengthen the coast defences, a new Revenue force was established in 1809 called the Preventive Waterguard (the name survived in the Customs and Excise until the early 1970s). This body of men was intended to link up with the existing forces – the cutters and the maligned riding officers. The new force would operate near to the shore and tackle the smugglers that had managed to run the gauntlet of the cutters further out to sea. The Waterguard, as the name suggests, were provided with small rowing galleys to patrol the shores regularly. The new 'preventive men' were normally stationed away from their homes to avoid any collusion with relatives and friends. Therefore accommodation had

31

to be found for them and as no local people were prepared to board them, the Customs Board were forced to purchase land to build 'preventive stations'. These were the precursors of the Coastguard cottages, many of which are still standing today. The coastline of England and Wales was divided into three districts, each controlled by an Inspecting Commander, who had overall command of the Waterguard and the cutters in the area. The three Commanders were selected from the most experienced cutter commanders. The new system was designed to provide a cohesive control of all the anti-smuggling forces – the Customs were beginning to get their act together.

During the next few years there were the first signs of a gradual change in smuggling methods. Reports, isolated at first, of smuggled goods being hidden in specially concealed compartments on vessels. This trend became more and more prevalent over the next 30 years as the old romantic type of smuggling runs on the shore became less and less frequent. Although it must be stressed that the change did not come overnight, the move to what some writers have called 'the scientific period' was slow and there were still many bitter battles to be fought both on land and sea.

The ending of the French war brought fresh problems for the Revenue service. Over a quarter of a million soldiers and sailors were discharged, all well versed in the arts of warfare and with little encouragement to settle down to gainful and honest employment, even if such could be found. The Treasury and the Customs expected a rise in smuggling and they were not to be disappointed. However, the Customs Board were shocked and dismayed at the Treasury's solution to the anticipated problem.

With effect from February 1816 the Preventive Waterguard was taken away from the Customs and placed under the control of a Royal Navy Captain, who was given strict orders to reorganise the Service on naval lines and to introduce naval discipline. Recruitment for the Service was placed in the hands of the Admiralty. The Admiralty was also given control of all the cutters. The timing of this radical change was perfect for the Admiralty Board, embarrassed by the number of unemployed officers on half pay, or 'on the beach' in Navy parlance. This vast reservoir of trained and battle-hardened men could be utilised as commanders and mates of the cutters. But the Customs and Excise services were rendered virtually devoid of any anti-smuggling forces.

Furthermore the Treasury accepted a proposal put forward by the Admiralty for a 'Coast Blockade' of the Kent coast. This plan was really the brain child of Captain Joseph McCulloch, R.N. as the only real solution to the smuggling problem. The autocratic Captain had scant regard for Revenue officers, he felt that they were lax, inefficient and invariably in league with the smugglers. The Coast Blockade involved the establishment of a number of blockade stations manned by seamen, each station commanded by a Naval lieutenant. Each stretch of coast between the blockade stations would be patrolled day and night. McCulloch commanded the new force from a ship of the line anchored in the Downs and the Martello towers, built for another kind of invasion which did not materialise, housed the Blockade men.

By the 1840s the coastguard depicted here on a cigarette card had become essentially a naval reserve.

After just one year of operation the Blockage was extended to the Sussex coast. McCulloch was a strict disciplinarian – not for nothing was he known as 'Flogging Joey'. He imposed a strict, even harsh, regime over his men, this added to the uncongenial living conditions and the dangerous nature of the work made it difficult to recruit the right type of seamen. Quite soon the Blockade Service was manned by the scum of the Navy, the Blockade men or 'warriors', as they were called, were universally hated and they were destined to be involved in some of the most bitter battles in smuggling history.

It is interesting to note that a more famous Naval Captain had similar thoughts on the 'blockade solution'; but perhaps it is not so

33

surprising as the Navy had successfully blockaded many French and Spanish ports during the war. Captain Frederick Marryat, later to gain fame as a best selling author, had been employed on Revenue duties off the Devon coast. His views on smuggling were expressed in a long memorandum to the Admiralty. He, too, considered the whole Preventive Service inefficient and badly organised and felt that if 'revenue cruisers were not at anchor so much, there would be less incidence of smuggling.' His ultimate solution was a complete blockade of the smuggling ports such as Dunkirk, Cherbourg and Roscoff. In his opinion, 'the cruisers would have a far better chance of falling in with the smugglers than when dispersed over a wide area of coast.' His plan was almost tantamount to outright war again and was not seriously considered by the Admiralty.

There was no doubt that the new measures were having their desired effect and achieving some moderate success. But it was at a great financial cost. Nearly 7,000 persons were employed in the various forces at an annual expense of well over a half a million pounds. There was also a certain lack of co-operation between the forces with many instances of duplication of effort. The Treasury, ever keen to obtain value for money, felt it was high time to re-examine in detail the various services involved in the prevention of smuggling. Never had one subject been so deliberated or taxed the minds of so many public servants.

The Committee appointed to study the problem expressed its concern at 'the most flagrant degree of audacity and violence of the smugglers' and the 'considerable quantities of spirits and tobacco introduced from the other side' – not particularly original comments as it had all been said many times before. However, they did think that most of 'the silks, laces, gloves etc had been brought in clandestinely by individuals arriving in the packets or in trading vessels' – the first admission by a Government committee that passengers did smuggle! The Committee expressed grave misgivings at the lack of central control of all the preventive services and it had doubts about the efficiency and loyalty of the Coast Blockade Service. The Committee recommended that the Preventive Water-guard be returned to the control of the Customs Board, the force of riding officers be reduced to a mere 50 men and all but the largest Revenue cutters also returned to Customs control.

The report was approved and with effect from 15th January 1822 the new preventive establishment – the Waterguard, the cutters and the riding officers – were amalgamated into one force under a new name, 'The Coast Guard' (the two words were separate for a number of years). Though the force was under the direction of the Customs Board, it was headed by a Royal Navy Captain – William

Bowles – and in future all the officers and men appointed to the Coastguard were nominated by the Admiralty, thus establishing the now long tradition of Naval principles. Despite the doubts the Coast Blockade Service survived.

Indeed it was that service especially that was involved in frequent battles with armed smugglers, often more than 200 in number. Between 1821 and 1824 five officers were killed and over 30 seriously injured with countless more suffering 'minor cuts and broken limbs'! One of their main opponents in Kent was the Aldington gang, also known as 'The Blues' – the last of the big organised gangs. They were finally captured in 1826 and stood trial at Maidstone (all, according to the report, in the 'universal smuggler's smock'). The judge's comments on passing the death sentence – later commuted to transportation – showed the difference in outlook and opinion since the days of the previous century when smuggling was condoned as an honest and romantic form of criminal activity. His words were,

> '. . . pleaded guilty to an offence of a most heinous nature, which struck terror into every well-disposed mind. It must be made known throughout the country that if an offence of this nature were again committed no mercy would be shown to the offenders. . . . If persons in the highest stations of life were not to purchase smuggled goods there could be an end to smuggling, but many people laboured under the delusion that defrauding the revenue was no crime. It was a serious offence against the laws of God and smuggling led to the Commission of the greatest crime that of murder.'

With such an outright condemnation the days of large scale smuggling were numbered.

The last important run occurred in 1829 when a large band of smugglers conveyed a train of carts and horses loaded with spirits and tobacco through the streets of Lydd in broad daylight. It was reported that the townspeople gathered to cheer the smugglers – little did they realise that they were witnessing the passing of an era. The battle had largely been won, at least sufficiently to disband the Coast Blockade Service in 1831 when the Coastguard took over their duties.

The encouraging early success of the Coastguard forced the smugglers to resort to more ingenious methods to hide and land their goods. The wooden sailing vessels were particularly well suited to a variety of concealments – hollow bulkheads, false bows, double bottoms in cabins, false ceilings, as well as goods being hidden in coils of rope, sails, in cargo and in ballast. It was also reported that Deal fishermen (Deal again!) concealed tea and tobacco in specially fitted 'corsets', 'bustles', 'thigh pieces' and in 'cotton bags to fit the crown of a hat'. Vessels in the purely coasting trade were suspect as they rendezvoused with French vessels and concealed the smuggled goods under cargoes of coal and grain. One vessel was built as two vessels one within the other, the large space used to conceal a great quantity of tobacco. Another vessel seized by a Revenue cutter off Cornwall had concealments in double bulkheads, in the coal locker, false forepeak, false flooring in the hold and false ceilings in the cabins; over 320 ankers of spirits were hidden and all the bulkheads and decking had been newly tarred so that the smell of spirits should not be apparent.

The most popular stratagem was to sink spirit tubs close to the shore attached to a recovery line, which was marked by a small buoy. This operation was called 'sowing the crop'. In an attempt to counter this ploy one of the regular duties of the Revenue boats was to patrol the shore using grappling irons in the hope of locating the sunken goods. This duty was known as 'creeping' and was most unpopular with the crews; it was time-consuming, very tedious and largely non-productive.

And as for smuggling by passengers, this trade appeared to be flourishing if judged by some of the goods seized by Customs officers at Dover in the 1830s. The variety of goods is really quite amazing: silk stockings, chips (for hats), lace, silk cravats, snuff boxes, ink-stands, earrings, leather gloves, clocks, wineglasses, eau-de-Cologne, petticoats, 'manufactured hair', playing cards, musical boxes, silk umbrellas, cambric petticoats, fans, necklaces, perfumery, porcelain, lace veils, vultures' feathers, porcelain teeth, musical instruments, endless articles of silk and lace clothing and not to mention tea, tobacco and French brandy. In those days each vessel had to produce a passenger list and when the passengers landed they were shown into a waiting room and were called forward individually to clear their baggage – many complained of 'the long delays in draughty warehouses'. Then there was no such thing as 'passenger concessions', duty was paid on all goods obtained abroad; it was not until 1850 that an allowance of ½lb tobacco was granted duty-free and extended to include spirits in 1875. The Customs officers complained, 'Lady passengers are dressing themselves in valuable dresses and jewels, more calculated for their entry into a drawing room, than merely to come ashore. They are all items newly acquired abroad.' The steady rise of petty smuggling by passengers would continue during the century as foreign travel became no longer a privilege of the nobility and upper classes. The Chairman of the Customs Board thought, 'it would be very unfair to call upon parties to declare whether they had goods liable to duty or not, and to subject them to a severe penalty if they made a false declaration'. A fine example of Victorian dual morality – 'ordinary' smugglers were still liable to be transported for very minor smuggling.

Although *Punch* magazine described the Coastguard stations as, 'Castles of idleness where able bodied men spent their time looking through long glasses for imaginary smugglers'(!) this was far from the truth. The conditions of service were arduous, the hours were long and the discipline was strict. The men were continually reminded that their sole responsibility was the protection of the Revenue. Any suspicion of collusion with the smugglers was harshly punished. One rather unfair order was promulgated that a list would in future be kept of every person serving at a station, within which a smuggling run had taken place. Officers and men placed on this list would not be considered eligible for promotion or entitled to any indulgence or favour. This was Naval discipline with a vengeance.

In 1831 it was suggested that the Coastguard should become 'in all its branches essentially Naval'. From this time on all new recruits were trained at Naval establishments and were required to serve on Naval vessels abroad if necessary. It thus became in essence a Naval reserve force with the prevention of smuggling becoming a secondary consideration. Indeed during the Crimean War over half its officers and men saw active service. At the same time the organisation of the riding officers – now known as the Mounted Guard – was drastically altered. All new entrants were to be aged under 30 years and also to have had experience in a cavalry regiment. Their numbers were greatly reduced until they were a mere handful of men stationed at the old notorious smuggling areas – Deal, Folkestone, Hastings, Isle of Wight, Swanage and Fowey.

One of the features of the period was the great improvement in the information the Coastguard received about the movements of smuggling vessels. Some Revenue vessels were sent on 'intelligence runs' to reconnoitre the many French ports, where men were landed to note details of vessels loading likely cargoes. However, the main source of intelligence were the so-called 'correspondents' in the various ports. They were possibly English merchants resident in the ports, some were quite definitely paid informers. They produced a wealth of detailed information on names of vessels, ports to which they belonged, names of masters, and even precise quantities of goods being loaded. This valuable information was only of real value to the cutters operating off the south-west coast because of the longer crossing time, which enabled the information to filter through. If these reports are to be believed, and there is no reason to doubt their

37

'Creeping' – a task hated by the Preventive Service. As shown on this cigarette card, small fluked grapnells were dragged along which hooked on to sunken contraband.

veracity, there was still a very flourishing trade between Cherbourg and Roscoff and Cornwall and Devon. As a sign of the changing climate more information on smuggling runs was being received from informers in the various English ports.

The battle at sea between the cutters and the smuggling vessels had changed quite dramatically to one of a 'cops and robbers' chase. The majority of smugglers no longer sought to fight it out with cutters but mostly turned tail to avoid capture. The smuggling vessels often would jettison their illegal cargo, not solely to lighten the vessel for extra speed but also to avoid being caught red-handed. Even if subsequently they were apprehended by the Revenue it was very difficult to prove in a court of law that the recovered cargo had in fact come from the captured vessel.

The smuggling trade at this time gives the overall impression of a game of hide and seek played on a grand scale. The smugglers attempted to gain information on the timing of Coastguard patrols and the movements of cutters – in fact several Coastguard men were court-martialled for passing on such information for gain. Whilst the Revenue men, or 'Philistines' as they were now commonly called, were desperately trying to buy information on the smugglers' movements. One could say that smuggling had become civilised.

There can be no doubt that the Coastguard and its force of cutters – nearly 50 in number – and ably abetted by the Customs officers at the ports were achieving a very marked success. The quantity of seized goods had increased especially during the late 1830s. However, despite the obvious increased efficiency and better returns, the greatest single factor in the reduction of smuggling was the steady lowering of import duties and the introduction of free trade. Back in the 1770s Adam Smith had stoutly maintained that the only answer to smuggling was the reduction of punitive duties and at long last his views were being vindicated.

The leading proponent of 'laissez-faire' was Sir Robert Peel. This politician is more remembered these days for the foundation of the first police force. However, Sir Robert was an ardent believer in the removal of all trade barriers and the reduction of restrictive import duties. He had a very low opinion of the Customs service; he distrusted it utterly and was convinced that many of its officers were dishonest and few had been very vigilant. With hindsight his view was somewhat justified as during the next few years several large-scale frauds were uncovered in the London docks. However, it is doubtful whether this mistrust influenced his policy on free trade nor indeed is there evidence that Peel took smuggling into consideration when he embarked on his programme of tariff reform.

In the four years from 1842 to 1845 no less than 1,200 dutiable articles were freed from duty. The repeal of the restrictive and unpopular Corn Laws in 1846 ensured that Great Britain would essentially become a free trade country. Indeed it was the firm conviction of politicians, merchants and industrialists that 'laissez-faire' was the cornerstone of the buoyant prosperity of mid-Victorian Britain – as epitomised by the Great Exhibition of 1851. By this year only 48 articles were liable to import duty and ten years later a trade treaty signed with France drastically reduced the duties on French wines and brandy as well as exempting many French goods.

The only articles that brought in any appreciable revenue were sugar, tobacco, tea, wines, coffee and timber. So henceforth the smuggler was left with only these goods to trade as the illegal trade in tea, wines and silks virtually ceased when the profit margin became not really worth taking the increased risks. Sugar was not a commodity that lent itself easily to smuggling and it had never featured much even in the heyday of smuggling. The only goods which remained worth smuggling were spirits and tobacco. Spirits, largely because of their bulk and smaller profitability, were smuggled far less; for the remainder of the 19th century the main, and almost only, commodity of the smuggler was tobacco.

A report, issued in 1844, on the conditions of the tobacco trade alleged that, 'a considerable amount of tobacco is daily brought into the Country and can be obtained anywhere for 2s 6d per lb' (the duty alone was 3s 2d per lb!). Much of the smuggled tobacco was brought ashore by ships' crews. Indeed it was suggested that many shipping companies deliberately kept the seamen's wages low as 'they all have the power to make a venture'. For some unaccountable reason the north-east appeared to be the most notorious area for tobacco smuggling. In 1843 over 15,000 lbs was seized in the Tynemouth area and on the Humber nearly 20,000 lbs. The tobacco appeared to come from Holland, Belgium, Prussia and America. One large London tobacco manufacturer maintained that in excess of 20 million lbs of tobacco was smuggled into the country each year, although this does seem a rather gross exaggeration. Certainly the Thames estuary came into its own with tobacco being landed from Leigh in the east right up to the Pool of London. Several seizures of tobacco were made being landed within sight of the London Custom House in Lower Thames Street!

There is a story that one of the main receivers of smuggled tobacco in London was a 'Mother Gregson', who kept a chandler's shop in Barking churchyard. It was reputed that her shop was a front and was in reality 'a clearing house for smuggled goods' and that she acted as an agent for many large London tobacco merchants. Her carriers were young boys – all under the age of 16 years and thus free from prosecution. She seems to have stepped straight out of a Dickens novel – a female Fagin!

All vessels arriving at the ports were suspect. Tobacco was concealed on board regular trading vessels, either in the accommodation or in the holds, although with the coming of steam vessels, the engine room became a favourite place. With so many goods now duty-free one of the tricks was to hide tobacco in duty-free goods. Coasting vessels, which normally received scant attention from the Customs, were greatly involved in the trade. The tobacco was overstowed by bulk cargoes like coal, grain, apples and fish. The tobacco was either obtained by making a quick trip across to the Continent on route to the coasting port or by buying direct from Dutch vessels hovering just outside the limits. These vessels were virtually floating tobacco shops and it was thought that there were at least two dozen of them operating along the east coast, which is not really surprising as their market seemed boundless – no less than 25,000 coasters and collier vessels used the Thames estuary every year.

Jersey and Guernsey were still in the illegal trade, supplying large quantities of tobacco to vessels trading along the south coast. One of the features of the Channel Isles trade was the way tobacco was packed to resemble other goods. The Customs in Portsmouth seized a quantity of tobacco from Jersey, which was cut into pieces exactly resembling shoe soles. And often the tobacco was packed in rolls to appear like old rope. Ports on the southern Ireland coasts were deeply involved in the tobacco trade, the goods coming all the way from America. Figures suggested that a shipment of 50,000 lbs of American tobacco could bring a net profit of over £3,000. This calculation allowed for the loss of 'decoy bales' (to be left for the

Revenue to seize) and bribes to the Coastguard! There were also many reports of smuggling runs where, 'the country people muster in large numbers armed with sticks, pitchforks, and scythes to help the smugglers. Not one of these will incriminate the purchaser'. Smuggling was not yet completely dead!

In 1851 Collectors at every port in the Kingdom as well as all Inspecting Commanders of the Coastguard were requested to report on the extent of smuggling in their areas over the previous ten years, with any observations they cared to make on the state of the trade. There had been 70 large scale smuggling runs over the decade – on average seven a year – throughout the whole of the country, including Scotland and Ireland. In nearly one third of these runs most of the goods were recovered, many smugglers were arrested and quite a few vessels, carts and horses seized. These figures present a picture of a declining trade.

These returns give an excellent and accurate picture of the state and extent of smuggling at the middle of the century. One surprising feature, which they disclose, is how the trade varied from coast to coast. No longer could it be said that smuggling was endemic to any stretch of coast, as it had been less than 30 years ago, now it would appear that the problem was not nationwide but had become localised and thus somewhat easier to control and contain.

As was to be expected the Collectors and the Coastguard were in broad agreement that tobacco smuggling was on the increase on the north-east. The problem with the collier vessels has already been noted and added to this were the Scandinavian vessels bringing timber to most of the Tyne ports. At Whitby the French fishing vessels that gathered in great numbers during the herring season were causing great concern. Further south on the Humber things had improved, no doubt brought about by some notable seizures by the Customs at Hull; over 40,000 lbs of tobacco had been seized, several runs on the Yorkshire coast frustrated and more than 300 people convicted of smuggling. The collector at Hull could afford to be smug when he reported, 'smuggling has been materially checked in this district.'

The east coast from Grimsby down to Harwich, which had been in the forefront of the trade in earlier times was now particularly quiet. The explanation given was, 'the zeal and vigilance of the Coast Guard and the cutters, which has resulted in substantial losses sustained by the smugglers has considerably checked the illicit trade'. At Harwich the only problem was the continued smuggling by packet boat crews, though all were of 'a petty nature' and it was ever so!

Perhaps the most surprising disclosure was that in Kent and

Sussex, the hot-bed of smuggling for so many centuries, the trade had so diminished that soon 'it will be completely extinct'. The reasons for this quite amazing *volte-face* seemed to be that the coast was now too well guarded to hold out any reasonable hope of success, and that a recent Act of Parliament had made foreigners liable to the same penalties as Englishmen if caught smuggling. This legislation was not before time, for too many years Revenue officers on the cutters had been frustrated when capturing smuggling vessels to find that the majority of the crew were shown as either Frenchmen or Dutch despite having names such as 'O'Connor', 'Kelly', 'O'Leary', and the like! Hitherto foreign nationals were not liable to prosecution under the existing smuggling legislation, nor indeed could foreign vessels be seized. At Dover the concern was, 'the accession of wealthy passengers to the smuggling company' and for the first time foreign watches were being smuggled in large numbers.

As a direct antithesis to the general improvement in the rest of the country, the Revenue officers along the coasts of Hampshire, Dorset and the Isle of Wight were deeply concerned at the very apparent increase of smuggling in their areas. In Portsmouth a new system of smuggling was being tried. Rafts of ankers of spirits were lashed together and allowed to float in on the tide, to be collected later by means of a drag line affixed to two grapnels on the 'raft'. As one Coastguard official commented, 'such is the desperation of the trade in this area'. The upsurge of the trade at Weymouth was said to be caused by the increase of population on 'the Island of Portland consequent of the formation of a harbour of refuge as well as the convict establishment'. Portland and the Chesil Beach remained an infamous smuggling area until the latter decades of the century. It was in this area that Falkner, the author of *Moonfleet*, the most reputable smuggling novel, grew up surrounded by tales of smuggling and shipwreck. The Isle of Wight was a problem in itself; it was considered that, 'the people of the Isle are very much more addicted to smuggling than is generally supposed.' The Customs Collector at Cowes was even more trenchant in his comments, 'the whole population are smugglers . . . here are fishermen, who do not fish . . .' The island remained the last bastion of 'old style smuggling' with runs of tobacco and spirits being landed well into the 1870s. Tradition would seem to die hard on the island.

Those once great centres of the smuggling trade – Devon and Cornwall – were now almost inactive, or at least relatively so. This strange state of affairs had been brought about by 'the active exertions of the Coast Guard and the number of cutters that regularly patrol the coasts'. Indeed the sudden appearance in the mid 1840s of the first Revenue steam cutter, rather well named

Vulcan, made quite an impression on the local smugglers, who no doubt felt that the use of a steam cutter was gaining a very unfair advantage over them! Famous smuggling ports such as Falmouth, Fowey, Gweek, St Ives, Padstow and Dartmouth had become so 'legal' that it was intimated that the Coastguard might be withdrawn 'without danger to the Revenue'. Perhaps that was a slight exaggeration but my, how times had changed!

The Bristol Channel and the Welsh coasts were at long last properly guarded and the decrease of smuggling in these areas was attributed to 'the presence and diligence of a strong force'. A note of caution was expressed that 'no part of the coast of England (and Wales?) affords greater facilities for smuggling ... and therefore it needs constant supervision'. One could comment that such a statement is not out of place today. Liverpool had a smuggling trade all of its own. It had been brought about by the phenomenal growth of the port and its trade, which was now second only to London in importance. In the previous five years there had been no less than 3,000 seizures of tobacco goods, all found concealed on board or smuggled ashore by ships' crews. The Collector felt that the situation was controllable, especially as 'runs on the coast are things of the past'.

In Scotland, where smuggling was at a very low ebb, the Revenue vessels and the Excise were deeply involved in a much different problem – the illicit distillation of spirits. The same applied to Ireland. Though the collector in Dublin felt that tobacco smuggling was still carried on to a serious extent because 'the Coastguard service in Ireland was far from what it should be'! However, he was obviously not aware of the desperate state of the rest of the country, where 'the poverty of the people and the sickness of 1849 coupled with the recent extensive emigration had virtually extinguished the smuggling trade.' Indeed such was the state of the country that Revenue cutters were used to take food and coin to some of the more remote coasts on the west of the island in a desperate attempt to alleviate the effects of 'the Great Hunger'.

One of the last big seizures of smuggled goods was made in December, 1849 at Sea Reach in the Thames Estuary. *Vigilant*, one of the most famous Revenue cutters of all time, stopped and searched a sailing barge named the *Charlotte* and found 14,402 lbs of tobacco hidden in its holds. Although the seizure was said to have been made without information, it seems more than a coincidence that the cabin boy of the *Charlotte* had the same Christian name and surname as one of the *Vigilant*'s mariners. Fortunately this final reminder of the old smuggling days was captured for posterity in a fine engraving of the scene.

43

The Coastguard in 1850 comprised over 6,000 men and had no less than 70 cutters of various sizes operating around the coasts – all at an annual cost of over a half a million pounds. The review of smuggling throughout the Kingdom suggested that some reduction could be made in the size of the service without greatly endangering the Revenue. There was a sharp reduction in the land force and over a quarter of the cutter fleet was disbanded. In 1854 with the outbreak of the Crimean War over 3,000 Coastguard men were drafted into the Navy and their places were filled by Naval pensioners and many of the remaining cutters were seconded to the Royal

44   *Smugglers Alarmed*, a popular print of the early 19th century.

Navy. Despite this fact and the depletion of the guard around the coasts, there was no evidence of any increase of smuggling during the period. It was now recognised that the protection of the Revenue against smuggling was only one of the many reasons for the existence of the Coastguard. The defence of the coasts in case of invasion, acting as a Naval reserve and its life saving duties were all considered more important than the anti-smuggling aspect. In 1856 it was therefore decided to transfer the control of the service from the Customs to the Admiralty. The Customs Board made very strong representations to the Treasury on the wisdom of such a change. However, they were informed that the responsibility rested solely with the Government and the Customs Board would stand 'entirely exonerated, if any inconvenience arose to the detriment of the Revenue'. Thus, in short, if smuggling increased as a result it would not be the Customs' fault! From 1856 no Customs officer has carried arms though the Coastguard men remained armed for many years to come in their role of 'defence of the coasts'.

Despite all their previous misgivings the Customs Board were able to report in the following year,

> 'With the reductions of duties and the removal of needless and vexatious restrictions, smuggling has greatly diminished and the public sentiments with regard to it have undergone a very considerable change. The smuggler is no longer an object of public sympathy or a hero of romance, and people are just beginning to awake to the perception of the fact that his offence is less a fraud on the Revenue, than a robbing of the fair trader. Smuggling proper is now almost entirely confined to tobacco, spirits and watches . . . all these cases are on the decrease and in the last ten years have diminished to about one-third.'

Thus although smuggling had not ceased, it had been greatly reduced and what remained was emerging in a completely different format. The long battle that had been waged over the last two centuries had finally been won – 'The gentlemen had gone by'!

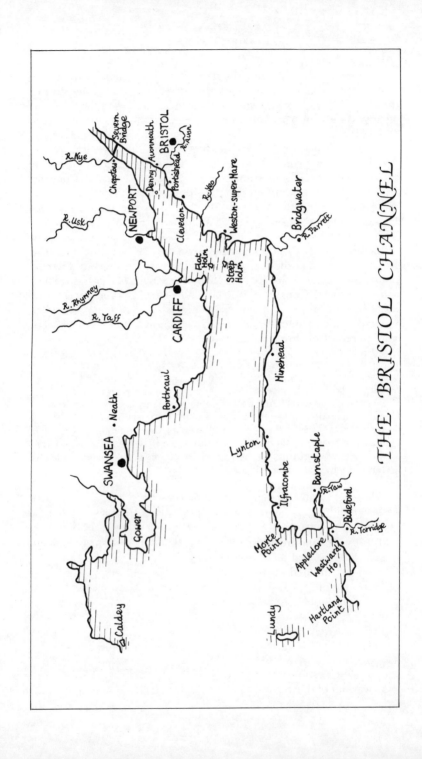

THE BRISTOL CHANNEL

2
The Impact Along The Bristol Channel

The Bristol Channel is the largest and longest inlet along the whole of the British coastline. From time immemorial it has been an important waterway – the gateway to the western seas. For centuries it has figured large in the maritime history of the country; Cabot, Grenville and Brunel are just a few names that come instantly to mind.

However, its name is of relatively recent origin; the first appearance in any map of the name 'Bristol Channel' was in a famous sea-atlas published in Leyden about 1584 when it was shown as 'De Canel van Brostu', which shows the importance of the port of Bristol at that time. The new name replaced the earlier 'Severn Sea' to which Leland gave many references in his *Itinerary*. This earlier name sounds more romantic and evocative and it has been perpetuated by writers and poets ever since.

The number of Iron Age hill forts that are dotted along its coasts evince a considerable trading presence long before the Romans came. There are many tales of strange craft manned by even stranger mariners arriving with goods from the Orient, which were then traded by barter.

As Chesterton wrote, the Romans arrived 'striding out to Severn', though they knew the estuary as 'Sabrina'. They used the seaway to transport the lead from the Mendips and the gold mined from the Welsh hills as well as a supply route for the numerous forts and settlements situated in the hinterland.

During the Dark Ages when the eastern seaboard was beset by Saxons, this western sea-route maintained a tenuous link with the Continent and the Mediterranean and fostered the trade links with Ireland – albeit, at first, in the export of slaves! It was along this waterway that the Celtic missionaries proceeded (some by coracle) to spread Christianity, establishing their rudimentary churches along both its shores.

It was out of this Severn Sea that the first intrepid sailors set forth into uncharted waters in a brave search for the New World. Many West Country seamen were in the vanguard of seeking new trade routes. They were followed later by settlers to the new colonies in North America. These early pioneers established historic trading links with Newfoundland and the Americas, which brought wealth and prosperity to the Channel ports.

All estuaries are natural entries for invaders and the names of Lundy and the two Holms are constant reminders of the regular Viking incursions and depredations along the Severn Sea. They were followed by Barbary pirates, Sallee rovers, dreaded 'Biscayers' and Spanish privateers as well as Cornish 'pyrates from Fowey'. These pirates, whatever their creed, colour or nationality used Lundy Island as a base and found the wealth of shipping in this stretch of waterway a rich source of plunder, so much so that Bideford Bay was also known as the 'Golden Coast'. They certainly brought a real and added danger to what was already a very treacherous coast for shipping. Even as late as 1636 four Turkish ships had entered the Bristol Channel and in a short space of time plundered 22 vessels. It was not until the 1660s that the Channel was declared to be free of pirates, only to be shortly replaced by smugglers, but more of that anon. Indeed in 1797 a squadron of French vessels appeared in the Channel off the North Devon coast. Their arrival caused some consternation and fears of an invasion. They did some damage to Ilfracombe before landing near Fishguard. There they were soundly defeated by the local militia and the crews of two Customs cutters – the last invasion of this country by foreign troops.

The rise and fall of many of the Bristol Channel ports accurately reflects the fluctuating history of maritime trade. Bideford and Barnstaple grew first out of the wool trade of Exmoor and as this declined they found an even richer substitute in tobacco, which brought a short-lived prosperity to these two ancient river ports. Indeed it is reputed that Raleigh landed the very first bale of tobacco onto the Strand at Bideford. Further up the Channel both Watchet and Minehead were busy and important ports – Watchet is slowly recovering some past glories but Minehead is now more famous as a holiday resort.

The major port of the Channel for centuries was Bristol. It can trace its origins back to the 11th century. Some years later a contemporary historian commented, 'Many sayle to Bristowe'. By 1500 it was the metropolis of the Bristol Channel, it attracted trade from all the ports of the Channel – large and small alike. Its direct trade with the Continent and Ireland made it second only in importance to London. Unfortunately soon after this it suffered a period of depression, only for its fortunes to be revived by the development of trade with the Americas and West Indies. By the end of the 18th century the port was fast losing ground to Liverpool and soon it faced even sterner competition within the Channel area itself with the coal ports of Newport, Cardiff and Barry, whose rise to importance was nothing short of meteoric. During the coal boom the Bristol Channel was probably the busiest waterway in the country, if not in the world. In more recent times all the Channel ports have suffered as a result of changing trading patterns and cargo handling. River ports like Bristol, Bridgwater, Bideford and Barnstaple have virtually ceased as commercial ports; only those situated at the mouths of rivers have managed to survive – Avonmouth, Newport, Cardiff, Swansea and, of course, Royal Portbury – Bristol's answer to the changed trade.

Ship building once figured large in the Bristol Channel. Yards on the Taw and Torridge rivers provided many vessels in the days of Drake and Grenville but now Appledore is the only port to retain its ancient shipbuilding traditions. Bridgwater, too, was once a flourishing area; small ketches, schooners and sloops built in the numerous yards dotted along the river Parrett plyed their trade in the narrow seas during the sailing era. And, of course, Brunel's two great pioneer ships the *Great Western* and the *Great Britain* made their first voyages from the Cumberland Basin in the centre of the City, along the tortuous Avon and out into the Bristol Channel.

Two sailing vessels are, or rather were, unique to the Channel. The Severn trow – its name was derived from the Anglo-Saxon for a drinking vessel – was a double-ended open-decked barge with a very shallow draft ideally suited to the mud-flats and rivers of the upper reaches of the Channel. Trows were the ubiquitous working vessels of the Channel, they were used as the regular cross-channel 'market' boats carrying goods of all descriptions, passengers and cattle. Perhaps more famous and certainly more glamorous were the Bristol Pilot cutters. Built equally for strength and speed – they had to survive the fury of the Atlantic and the pilots were in fierce competition – these fine sea boats often sailed far beyond Lundy and the Bristol Channel looking for incoming vessels. They were considered the fastest working vessels of their time and the Bristol Channel pilots were the last to use sail to follow their trade.

The southern coast of the Bristol Channel from Hartland Point to Bridgwater Bay is an almost endless chain of reefs, rocks and

49

daunting vertical cliffs – it is just such majestic scenery that draws thousands of visitors every year. The Welsh coast, though not so fearsome, has its own perils to shipping, most notably the Gower coast. Therefore it is not really surprising that, facing the might and fury of the Atlantic, such 'cruel coasts' were a nightmare for mariners making their way up and down the Channel. One old Channel seaman remarked, 'Our Channel is a dreadful place – if you don't know your way about'. In the days of sail, especially, there were an endless number of 'spectacular' shipwrecks, Lundy Island was a particular navigational hazard. Many heroic rescues were made from lifeboat stations on both sides of the Channel. However, there are also many, many instances of wrecking and some are gruesome and fearsome tales indeed.

In at least one respect the Bristol Channel is a unique waterway, certainly as far as the British coast is concerned; it has one of the highest tidal ranges in the world (the vertical difference between high and low water). This also means that the rate of tidal flow is higher than normal for the British coast. It is quite usual for the flood tide to flow at three knots, increasing to six knots higher up the Channel and the ebb tide runs even stronger.

This tidal flow builds up and gains momentum around Lundy and then proceeds north-easterly producing a quite staggering tidal range which changes the vast mud-banks of rivers into full torrents

A Preventive Station. These were established the whole length of the Bristol Channel.

within a relatively short space of time. Twice a day places like Avonmouth and Beachley, where the banks of the Severn start to converge, have quite massive tides. This tidal flow brings masses of mud, sand and sediment, which has resulted in the number of dangerous sandbanks – another special feature of the Bristol Channel. The Channel's tides have meant added hazards for shipping and they have had some effect on the smuggling activities in the area.

As an added complication, during certain high tides the Channel tide rolls back the Severn waters, creating a bore – a tidal wave which at times can reach six feet or more. This wave rolls on most majestically back up the Severn and it provides a spectacular sight. It is interesting to note that there is a Government sponsored project to look at the various problems and consequences that would be caused by erecting a Severn Barrage – a proposal to turn the upper reaches of the Channel virtually into a lake by erecting a dam, possibly in the region of Weston-super-Mare. The tidal flow would then be harnessed to produce electricity. Such a proposal would not only be a massive engineering feat but it would transform the whole of the Channel coastline. The Bristol University project has been rather appropriately named 'Sabrina'.

One writer has suggested that the Bristol Channel 'is endowed with the intimacy of an inland sea' and that seems a very apt description for this important and fascinating waterway. The Channel has never been a barrier between the English and Welsh coasts – ports both large and small, traded freely with each other, almost on a daily basis; the Channel was one great marketplace with ports supplying each other's needs with facility. There were never any problems for passengers wishing to cross to the 'other side', market boats and ferry services being very regular; one is tempted to say that it was easier to cross the Channel in the 18th and 19th centuries than it was in modern times, before the advent of the Severn Bridge.

However, it was Bristol that was the hub of this inland sea, all ports traded with it and it became an entrepôt on a massive scale offering a world market to all the towns and ports in the area. For centuries Bristol could be considered the true capital of South Wales – a 'Welsh Emporium' as it was called in 1833; the quay called the Welsh Back and the old Welsh Market House are reminders of this past, when most of South Wales seemed geared to supplying Bristol's needs. Also most of the seaside resorts along the English coast (Weston-super-Mare, Clevedon and Ilfracombe are examples) largely developed as a result of the annual pilgrimage of holiday- 51 makers from the industrial South Wales.

The closeness of this inland sea is heightened by the fact that from each coast the opposite side is normally visible; on a fine, clear day the North Devon coast can be seen from the Gower almost 40 miles away. There is also a certain similarity in natural features between the two coasts. The estuaries of the Taw and Torridge equate with the Towy and Taf in Dyfed. The cliffs of the Vale of Glamorgan bear some relationship to the Quantocks, the lowlands or wetlands around Weston-super-Mare compare with the 'levels' of Gwent and the sand dunes of Ogmore are echoed by those around Braunton. These natural features of both coasts had quite a considerable bearing on the smuggling activities in the area, as we will see later.

But how is the Bristol Channel to be defined? Where does the fresh water of the Severn meet the salt water of the Channel? And where indeed does the Atlantic Ocean start?

There is an old West Country adage that says, 'The old bed of the Severn runs out at Lundy'. Indeed I think it is fair to say that Lundy stands almost as a bastion guarding the entrance to the Channel. From Hartland Point in North Devon, a line some 40 or so miles due north to Caldey Island and Manorbier on the Dyfed coast can be considered the seaward limit of the Bristol Channel. From thence westward it is the uninterrupted Atlantic until the shores of New-foundland. To define the easterly limits of the Channel is not so easy a task. Most geographers would place it seaward beyond the two Holms – an imaginary line drawn from Woodspring, north of Weston-super-Mare to Lavernock Point, some miles south of Car-diff.

However, for the purposes of this book I take the limits of the Bristol Channel to be Hartland in North Devon and the Gower on the Welsh side. And to the east I consider the Channel to be bounded by the quite magnificent and beautiful Severn Bridge; in other words from Aust (now famed as a motorway service station!) across the mile or so to the ancient port of Chepstow. As an ex-Newportonian I would strongly defend this definition. We *knew* that it was the Bristol Channel that we gazed out at from our Gwent hills. And certainly our 'sea' trips in the beloved Campbell paddle steam-ers to Clevedon, Watchet and Weston were 'across the Channel' and *not* 'over the Severn'! Let us not destroy those childish illusions! Arthur Machen writing from Caerleon said, 'Through a cleft one might see now and again a bright yellow glint of the Severn Sea and the cliffs of Somerset beyond.'

To understand the smuggling activities of any area, one needs to have some concept of how the various ports developed and what were the normal (legal) trade patterns. This is even more important with Bristol Channel smuggling because, unlike the south and east coasts of England where the distances to the coasts of France, Holland and the Channel Islands were quite short, the sea route from the French coast was long and fraught with dangers. To sail around Land's End and fight the Atlantic all along the North Cornish and Devon coast was not the easiest of tasks in the summer, let alone in the winter and we know that smuggling was not an activity solely conducted during the mid-year months. Such long and dangerous journeys would seem to militate against much smuggling activity in the Bristol Channel. However, this was not so, the Bristol Channel was a constant problem of control for Customs and Excise men on both the Welsh and English coasts. The *cris de coeur* of the various Customs collectors for the Channel ports were frequent and all bore the same message, 'the Channel is infested with smugglers'. Obviously the smuggling activities were not so extensive as those on the south and east coasts and generally they were of a different character, but nevertheless they were of a sufficient scale and extent to produce their own smuggling folk-lore.

Until the beginning of the 19th century the trading patterns of the majority of the Bristol Channel ports were almost exclusively those governed by its major port – Bristol. Its control of trade in the Channel was almost absolute, it acted as a magnet for the other numerous small ports in the Channel, who appeared to operate as mere satellites to serve Bristol. Bristol influence on the maritime life of the Channel was immense, such a domination of the seaway showed how appropriately it had been named. Bristol's quays and warehouses acted as a massive clearing house for the majority of imports and exports in the area.

The only ports that managed to survive independently of Bristol were those situated at the seaward limits of the Channel. Barnstaple and Bideford had long traded direct with Ireland and the Americas. Defoe commented in the 1720s that both ports have 'considerable and wealthy merchants who trade to most parts of the trading world'. However, by 1800 the ports were declining in importance. There was a long established rivalry between the two ports and Bristol. The Bristolians were rather derogatory about the sailors of the Taw and Torridge, they called them 'down-homers' – men who hugged the shores of their native coast and rarely left the Channel!

On the Welsh coast Carmarthen and Swansea had always been free from Bristol's influence. Though both ports freely traded with Bristol and there were frequent ferry services, they had developed a strong foreign trade and more especially with Ireland. Carmarthen was in sad decline but Swansea, and to a lesser extent Neath, were developing a foreign trade divorced from Bristol's dominance. Up until 1800 Swansea and Neath held a virtual monopoly in the shipment of coal and culm (coal dust) in the Channel. They traded coal and especially culm to virtually every small port along the length of the Channel coast. Culm was used in limekilns and there was a myriad of these sited along the North Devon and Somerset coast, indeed some of the ruins have still survived.

From the earliest days of the port Bristol merchants had established a trading link with Ireland. Fish, hides and corn were the first exports, later all manner of manufactured goods, wines, sugar and other colonial goods. There is even evidence of porter being exported to Dublin in the 1770s – talk about taking coals to Newcastle! The goods were mainly sent to Dublin, Cork and Waterford. In return Bristol received large quantities of foodstuffs, live cattle, timber, wool and linen yarn. Although other foreign trade was more important and profitable for the port, the trade with Ireland was over and above the most prolific.

Another of Bristol's ancient and long established trades was the importation of wines. In the Middle Ages these mainly came from Bordeaux and Gascony. In 1358 there was a record of a vessel with a cargo of Gascony wine being wrecked in the Channel and the wine was washed up on the shore near Portesheved (Portishead), where it was quickly 'carried off by various men' – wrecking does have long traditions on this coast. With the outbreak of the Hundred Years War the Bristol merchants had to look elsewhere for their wines and they found suitable alternatives from Spain and Portugal, hence was established the long and lasting trade links with these two countries and Bristol's fine reputation for 'sack' or sherry.

From the days of Cabot, Bristol vessels had regularly traded with the Newfoundland fisheries. Only a few vessels returned directly to their home port, most carried their cargoes of fish and whale oil to Spain and Portugal, then returned to Bristol with fruit, wines and Spanish wool for the West Country cloth industry.

Nevertheless the basis of Bristol's prosperity in the 18th century can be summed up in one word – sugar. The pattern of Bristol's triangular trade is now famous. Down to the coast of Africa with a varied cargo, then load slaves for the West Indian sugar plantation – mainly Jamaica, and there take on cargoes of sugar, molasses, rum and cotton for the return journey to Bristol. Trade with the American colonies was mainly direct to Virginia and South Carolina to bring back tobacco, cotton and rice. Bristol never really gained an ascendancy with tobacco imports. At first they lost out to Bideford and

Excise Cutters made occasional patrols in The Bristol Channel.

Barnstaple then later in the century Liverpool, Glasgow and Greenock became the main ports for imports of tobacco. Bristol was, of course, an important emigration port for those wishing to settle in the new colonies. Frequently these transatlantic vessels called at ports in Southern Ireland to take on stores and provisions for the long journey – thus perpetuating another link with Ireland.

Compared with such a wealth of foreign traffic all other ports in the Channel paled into insignificance. Ilfracombe had gained importance as a harbour of refuge along an otherwise dangerous and inhospitable coast. It had, at one time, strong trading links with Ireland, mainly importing wool for the cloth industry but this trade suffered as the cloth industry went into decline. The port's vessels were then relegated to mainly coasting traffic to Cornwall, Bristol and Carmarthen and Milford and for many years the port had a regular, almost daily, ferry service with Swansea.

Minehead had also come to prominence as a safe haven. Defoe remarked that it was 'the best port and safest harbour in all these

55

counties'. At this time the port was at its peak of influence with a substantial Irish trade and a quite prolific trade with the colonies. But by the end of the century the port was reduced to one trading vessel and a number of fishing boats; its trade had not been able to compete with Bristol. Like Ilfracombe the town found its salvation by developing into a rather exclusive holiday resort. Watchet, Minehead's near neighbour, had sunk from its former glories as a busy port to a few small vessels trading up and down the Channel.

Bridgwater, sited some miles up the winding river Parrett, managed to survive in the shadow of Bristol probably because it did not attempt to compete with its trade. Probably more than any other port along the Channel, Bridgwater relied on the quite phenomenal Channel tides and it was said that the height of the tide was a daily conversation topic in the town. The port, which like Bristol was in the centre of the town, had quite a reasonable foreign trade, importing hides from the American colonies for the leather industry of Yeovil and Taunton; it also imported valonin in great quantities, used for tanning leather. However, Bridgwater was famed for its bricks and tiles. Its vessels regularly traded to other ports in the Channel as well as further afield, and the cargoes they carried were invariably bricks, tiles, cider, pit-props for the Welsh mines, hay for the pit-ponies and Caerphilly cheese for the miners! They came back home with coal, culm and iron goods for its shipbuilding industry.

The ports on the 'opposite side' of the Channel – Chepstow, Newport, Cardiff, Aberthaw and Porthcawl – were of little consequence for the majority of the 18th century; they had relatively little foreign trade and merely seemed to serve Bristol. Of them all Chepstow had the most ancient lineage and could boast of days when cargoes of wine from Bordeaux and Portugal, fish from Iceland and timber from America came to the port's quays which nestled along the banks of the river Wye. Those days had, alas, passed and the port's future lay with the export of timber and, more especially, oak bark for tanning and most of these cargoes went to Dublin, Wexford and Cork.

Both Newport and Cardiff supplied market goods from their rich farming hinterlands to Bristol, but they did maintain direct trading links with Ireland. But it was the opening of the two canals linking the ports directly with the coalfields and ironworks of the valleys that drastically changed their fortunes. Within a couple of decades their trade had so escalated that the balance of maritime trade moved from Bristol to the Welsh coast. Soon the ports were exporting their coal and iron goods to all parts of the world and in their heyday – at the beginning of the 20th century – the Bristol Channel was one of the busiest waterways in the world.

Aberthaw, like Minehead which is virtually opposite it on the other side of the Channel, owed its importance as a port because it was the only safe and natural harbour on the Glamorgan coast. It was ideally situated to trade the farm products of the Vale of Glamorgan to Bristol and other Channel ports and it also provided limestone for the numerous lime kilns dotted all along the English coast. However, as soon as Cardiff began to develop as a major port it went into decline and little remains today of this old port. Porthcawl as a port suffered competition from Barry on one side and Port Talbot on the other, it still retained some fishing vessels but more successfully turned itself into a thriving holiday resort.

Thus the Bristol Channel ports had established regular trading links with Spain, Portugal, the West Indies, the American colonies and certainly more importantly with Ireland. But what effect, if any, did these trade patterns have on smuggling in the area?

It has been clearly established that there were no regular legal trade connections with the French Channel ports of Dunkirk, Boulogne, Calais and Cherbourg, then the leading centres of smuggling; nor indeed was there much contact with the Channel Islands, which were almost solely devoted to the smuggling trade throughout the 18th century. Very few Bristol Channel vessels ventured to these islands in search of legal cargoes, let alone illegal. There are a few isolated instances of small vessels from Newport, Cardiff, Bridgwater and Ilfracombe bringing back cargoes of potatoes but certainly not on a regular basis. So unlike other smuggling areas there was no tradition of legal trade to the acknowledged smuggling areas onto which profitable smuggling could be grafted. Therefore the smuggled goods which arrived on the Bristol Channel coasts had been obtained from other sources, and the answer was to be found in Ireland and the Irish sea.

There is no doubt that for virtually the whole of the 18th century smuggling along the western coasts from North Cornwall right up to the Solway Firth and beyond was largely in the hands of Irishmen or of vessels operated by smuggling companies based first in the Isle of Man and later in Ireland. These companies and their vessels held an almost complete monopoly of the smuggling operations in the western seas, the influence and power of their organisations were all embracing and could be likened to the Mafia, so complete was their control. This was the major difference of the smuggling activities in Wales and the West Country from that elsewhere. In other parts of the country smuggling was organised and financed from *within* the various areas and ports, the smuggling 'barons' living in or close to

57

the smuggling community. There is no evidence or even unconfirmed legends of similar figures in the Bristol Channel area. Therefore the smuggling runs in the Channel area were mainly of a
speculative nature and as a result much more difficult for the
Customs authorities to counter.

In the first half of the 18th century the Isle of Man had become a
virtual warehouse of tobacco, wines, spirits and tea just waiting to
be shipped illegally to the mainland. It was reported that 'ten to
twelve boats are seen in a fleet every week leaving the Island for
Whitehaven, Wales and the Bristol Channel'. It was also said that
every man, woman and child on the island was involved in some
capacity or other. The island was a perpetual nightmare for the
Revenue authorities, a major problem that appeared quite insoluble.
Indeed the few brave Revenue vessels that had the audacity to
confront the smuggling vessels usually had to retire severely mauled
and there were instances of Revenue crews being captured and
imprisoned on the island.

The island was in a unique position; geographically it was ideally
situated within an easy sailing distance of the English and Welsh
coasts. Moreover though it belonged to the Crown, it did not form
part of Great Britain as far as the law and taxation were concerned.
The Duke of Atholl, who held the lease to the island, had imposed
his own insular duties collected by his own 'Customs officers'. The

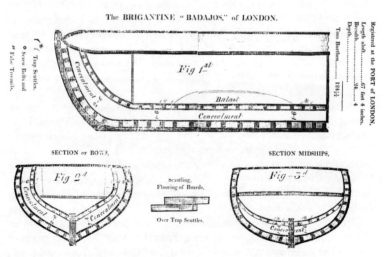

58   A very cunning method of concealment.

few duties that were in force were far lower than those on the mainland. Several large merchant houses had set up trading companies to exploit the situation and take advantage of the massive profits to be made in the illegal trade. The largest of these was Ross, Black & Christian, who bought enormous consignments of tea, tobacco and spirits purely for the smuggling trade.

In 1765 the British Government decided to purchase the island outright and with a nice sense of irony the funds for this purchase came from the Customs revenue! Customs officers were swiftly established there 'to prevent any illicit commerce'. In less than 20 years the Customs collector at Liverpool was bold, or unwise, enough to report, 'there has not been any information received of an avow'd smuggler coming within the limits of the port since the Purchase'. It is very unlikely that such a sweeping statement was correct; the presence of Customs officers on the island for such a short time would hardly have changed the lifetime habits of the islanders. However, what was evident was that the island's smuggling trade was never again so extensive, so to this end the purchase had been a success. Although the smuggling companies had not been broken up, they were forced to leave the island.

The place they selected as their new centre of smuggling operations was a small fishing port just north of Dublin called Rush; their choice was good, Rush was excellently placed to distribute their contraband goods the length and breadth of the western counties. The new centre was almost perfect as far as the Bristol Channel was concerned, as virtually every port in the Channel had some form of regular trade with Ireland and more especially with Dublin. As far as the Customs officials in the Channel ports were concerned every ship trading with Ireland had ample opportunity to obtain smuggled goods and therefore was suspect.

Although there was a Revenue Board in Ireland (it sat in Dublin), which administered and collected the Customs and Excise duties that were in force, it was not based on the English system and was not particularly efficient. It was not until 1801 and the Act of Union that the British system of collection of duties was introduced.

Port Rush became a smuggling entrepôt on a massive scale. There were four major smuggling companies based there and all were equally involved in the enterprise – John and James McCullogh, William Clancy, David Galwey & Co and Copinger & Co. These companies were not only the financiers but they were the masterminds behind most of the smuggling activities in the Irish Sea and the Bristol Channel. They had links with other merchant houses in English ports, notably Liverpool, and influential contacts on the

59

mainland. These smuggling entrepreneurs not only had their own smuggling vessels, they also financed 'free-lance' captains and of course, they sold goods to the masters of legally trading vessels, who had built up valuable contacts by regular trading to Dublin. These masters, though they could not be described as smugglers in the true sense of the word, often bought goods to specific orders from their 'customers' back in their home ports. They were able to do this because of the wealth and variety of goods held in the warehouses at Rush. Such a port acted as a magnet for adventurous seamen and the smuggling companies drew their captains from all over the country. Many were Welsh but the most notorious and fearless were Irish.

There is an old West Country saying that 'Smuggling money never did good to anyone.' And one old Cornish smuggler commenting on his experiences of the trade maintained, 'One moment there would be money and to spare, but it would be lost later on; and every smuggler that I remember died poor.' Now perhaps he was right but he was not speaking about these smuggling kings, their profits were enormous and their losses – certainly as far as the Bristol Channel was concerned – were minimal.

The main sources of smuggled goods to stock these warehouses were the Brittany ports of Nantes and Lorient, certainly as far as tea, spirits and wines were concerned. All of the Rush smuggling companies had their own establishments in Nantes and when that port's smuggling activities declined in favour of Roscoff on the northern coast they just moved their operations there also. It is quite amazing the amount of freedom and latitude these companies were given by the French authorities when one considers that for many years France was at war with England. Perhaps this may be explained by the affinity of the Bretons for other Celtic people – and after all the smuggling companies were de-facto Irish despite the fact that some of their members were quite obviously English. The French, of course, considered Ireland to be their ally and were quite prepared to help and encourage any activity that harmed the economic stability of England. There is no evidence that they supplied information to the French, although it is highly likely, but it is now thought that Copinger & Co might possibly have been passing information to the English Government! It was only during the early days of the French Revolution that the English and Irish smugglers were restricted as far as movement in France – they were suspected of helping the French aristocracy to escape.

The East India Company, who had a complete monopoly of tea, had several large warehouses in Lorient and they held regular auctions. During one week in 1766 it was recorded that Galwey & Co bought no less than 388 lots of tea. And in the years between 1768 to 1778 Copinger & Co had purchased almost four million pounds of tea and nineteen thousand barrels of brandy (these were large barrels not the ankers and half-ankers that were ultimately smuggled). The companies' vessels also regularly met the fleets of East Indiamen as they arrived in the approaches to the English Channel and they obtained from the masters and officers the more luxurious items of their trade – the silks, handkerchiefs and spices. One of the valuable perquisites of service with 'John Company' was that masters and officers were allowed cargo space to trade in their own right. The smuggling companies settled their bills with bankers' drafts drawn on London banks, such was their financial standing and reputation!

Strangely enough there are very few records of 'geneva' or gin being smuggled or seized in the Bristol Channel, though of course the source of most of the smuggled geneva was the eastern ports of France. However, the one spirit that seemed in plentiful supply was 'plantation' rum – in those days the colonies were known as the plantations. The amount of rum smuggled in the Bristol Channel suggests that supplies were not only obtained direct from West Indiamen returning up the channel to Bristol but that the larger consignments necessary to satisfy the trade were off-loaded quite legally at the southern Irish ports of Wexford, Cork and Kinsale. The Rush smuggling companies all had agents operating in these ports. Quite obviously the provisioning of Bristol vessels at these ports on their outward journeys had established valuable and trusted contacts, enabling the masters to buy speculative cargoes of rum and sugar for sale on their return voyages with or without the knowledge of their Bristol owners; though considering the strong independence of Bristol merchants I suspect the former to be more likely.

Tobacco was obtained in two distinct ways. The first was by obtaining supplies direct from the Bristol, Liverpool and White-haven vessels that traded with Virginia and Maryland. One cutter commander, whose Customs vessel was based at Milford, reported that 'the tobacco bum boats that meet the American ships are like bees round a honey pot and are just as elusive with a nasty sting when tackled!'. The second method, which was more common, was to obtain tobacco that had first been legally landed in England, warehoused and then exported duty-free. The trade in tobacco exported from Liverpool to Ireland was quite phenomenal. Indeed most of the tobacco that entered both Bideford and Barnstaple   61 during the early part of the century was intended for re-export to the Continent. Under the Navigation Laws no plantation goods could be shipped direct to the Continent, all had to come to England for onward transhipment. No doubt a fair percentage of this re-exported tobacco that left Bideford and Barnstaple never went far beyond the Bristol Channel, probably not much further than Lundy Island, before finding its way back into England without payment of duty. One Customs Collector suggested that within a week of exportation the tobacco was landed back on the mainland without payment of duty.

It is interesting to note that the generally accepted view was that smuggling vessels going to French ports to pick up cargoes of goods went in ballast, but there is evidence to show that many Irish smuggling vessels smuggled tobacco into France. Morlaix on the north Brittany coast had a virtual monopoly of tobacco manufacture in France. These Irish vessels ran a grave risk of jeopardising their privileged trading position in the French ports.

Another item that was frequently smuggled in the Bristol Channel was salt. It was a most valuable commodity, certainly in the 18th century when it was needed for preserving fish and meat but also used extensively in the leather industry. Most Channel ports had flourishing fishing fleets and those operating in Newfoundland waters needed large quantities of salt, and we have already remarked on the leather industry of Somerset. Salt had been liable to Excise duty ever since the introduction of the Excise and like most goods in the 18th century it was heavily taxed and cost, in England, between 4d to 5d per pound. However, in Ireland it could be obtained for 1d per pound or less, thus making it a most profitable item to smuggle. Much of the smuggled salt had been legally exported from Cheshire via the ports of Chester, Holyhead and Liverpool to Dublin and it was then smuggled back by mainly regular trading vessels, usually hidden under other cargo or ballast.

Soap was also smuggled in quite large quantities, if one can judge from the number of seizures made by the Customs. Again this was another commodity that carried a heavy Excise duty and by comparison was relatively cheap in Ireland. Dublin, like most cities, had a considerable soap industry and much of its production found its way into England and Wales. Bristol also had a number of soapmakers and there is evidence to show that exported soap never arrived at its intended foreign destinations, it was off-loaded to small coasting vessels further down the Channel and then re-landed duty-free.

62 Though smuggling in the Bristol Channel was predominantly the

preserve of Irishmen or Irish-based vessels from the Isle of Man and later Port Rush, they did not hold an utter monopoly of the trade. Certainly French smuggling vessels from Roscoff and Brest traded to the North Devon coasts but rarely went further up Channel, perhaps they were aware of the treacherous reputation of the Channel waters. Regular trading vessels from Spain and Portugal, both English and foreign, landed quantities of wines along the lower Channel coasts. In the 1730s a father and son partnership, Richard and Pasco Robinson, operated two vessels in tandem most success-fully; they smuggled goods from Guernsey which was their base. There are many references to Cornish smugglers coming further north than their usual haunts to land cargoes in the Channel, perhaps because they were becoming too well-known to the Revenue authorities along their own coast. Even the famous Carter family of smugglers from Prussia Cove near Penzance operated at times in the Channel. From Henry Carter's autobiography we read that he was well acquainted with the McCulloghs and William Clancey when they were based at Roscoff – maybe he ran some cargoes for them, though that is pure speculation. It does seem unlikely that 'The King of Prussia' as he was known, would undertake such work, such was his pre-eminence in the West Country smuggling fraternity.

Perhaps the one single feature of Bristol Channel smuggling that made it different to other areas, was the extent of smuggling under-taken by the regular small traders of the Channel – the market boats, the little colliers and the ferries – that criss-crossed over this 'inland sea' from port to port. This method of communication had been used for centuries so what was more natural than it should be used to distribute smuggled goods. On the odd occasion when the Customs did seize goods on these regular traders the quantities involved were quite trifling – the odd anker of brandy, a couple of pounds of tobacco and tea and a few bottles of wine – but the knowledge that smuggled goods were being moved in this manner made it most frustrating and their work almost impossible.

However, the main culprits in this trade were the Bristol Channel pilots. They had the greatest opportunities for trading as they met vessels coming into the Channel. Their vessels were very fast and could outsail the odd Revenue and Naval cutter that patrolled the Channel. Furthermore the pilots had an unsurpassed knowledge of the Channel tides and coasts. The Customs officials were convinced that 'most of the pilot boats are concerned in these illicit practices [smuggling]', but the Collector at Ilfracombe was adamant that four of the vessels, and he named them, were *entirely* employed in the running of goods onto the coasts; nevertheless few were ever caught 63

Persons dismissed from this Service cannot be employed in any other situation under the Customs or Excise.

SEIZURES.

EVERY Man employed in the Water-Guard is to make it his first, and most material *Object*, to secure the Person of the Smuggler. The Reward of 20*l.* granted for each Smuggler taken, or the Share of the Penalty recovered from him, will be paid (on the Certificate of the Inspecting Commander) to the Individual or Individuals by whom, or through whose means, the Smuggler is *absolutely* secured, and not to the Crew in general ; and it is to be distinctly understood, that although the Comptroller-General will consider as to the propriety of recommending to favourable consideration any Application for Reward on account of a Seizure lost by Endeavours to take the Smugglers, he will, in no case, overlook any Negligence, want of Courage, or Exertion, by which a Smuggler or Smugglers are allowed to Escape ; and unless Inspecting Commanders certify that the most active Exertions were made to take the Smugglers, no Reward for, or Share of any Seizure whatever will be paid or allowed.

The infamous 'Blood Money' instructions to the Coastguard in 1829.

red-handed.

The smuggling vessels that operated in the Bristol Channel tended to be much smaller in size than those in other smuggling areas. They were probably no larger than 50 tons on average and usually manned by 15 to 20 seamen and carried no more than six guns, though mostly just four. This made them small fry compared with the big smuggling luggers and cutters of the Kent, Sussex and Dorset coasts. Such small vessels were much more manoeuvrable in difficult waters and they were therefore well-suited to the sailing conditions found in the Channel. They were invariably described as 'Irish smuggling wherries' in the Customs records; and a wherry can be simply described as 'an open-decked sailing vessel with a very shallow draft' – ideal to negotiate the many mud-flats and sand-banks that exist in the Channel. Towards the close of the 18th century the smuggling companies invested in larger and faster vessels, ones which could compete on at least equal terms with the Revenue cutters that were just beginning to make their presence felt along the western seaboard. One such smuggling cutter that caused the Customs grave concern was the *Fox* of 90 tons captained by William Cullen of Rush, who was considered 'a most notorious smuggler'. The *Fox* was on the wanted list of all the Revenue vessels sailing in the western seas and despite several close shaves it was never captured.

However, the two names that figure most prominently in the smuggling exploits of the Bristol Channel were two brothers – John and Michael Connor. They both operated for Galwey & Co of Nantes and Rush. John, who was nicknamed 'Jack the Bachelor', was quite fearless and he has become an Irish folk-hero. He captained a small vessel called the *Mary Catherine*, which was just 16 tons and later the *Mary Elizabeth*, a slightly larger vessel at 28 tons. Despite the size of his vessels John Connor was quite prepared to take on larger Revenue cutters and one time fought two and escaped to tell the tale. In 1767 John was outlawed for his smuggling activities and was compelled to settle in Nantes, where not only did he organise the French end of the operations but also made the odd smuggling run into the Channel, as if 'to keep his hand in'! His brother operated his 28 ton *Bridget* with great success; though their names frequently appear in the Customs records neither brother was ever caught by the Revenue forces. Though fishermen by original occupation both could read and write, which was quite rare for those days; not only were the audacious smugglers but they were excellent seamen as well. To regularly and successfully trade from Nantes to the Bristol Channel in winter as well as summer in such small

65

vessels speaks volumes for their seamanship and courage. To contend with the Bay of Biscay and its notorious weather, navigate the rocky and dangerous Brittany coast, contend with the fury of the Atlantic and then survive the long haul up the North Cornish and Devon coasts was a daunting proposition, one that makes the relatively short cross-Channel route of the southern and eastern smugglers seem like an easy pleasure cruise by comparison. Even the route from Rush across the Irish Sea and St George's Channel could be more than hazardous at times. I think that the Connor brothers and their Irish colleagues must lay claim to be the most intrepid smugglers of their times.

As the Connors passed into folk and smuggling mythology so they were replaced by other names. Thomas Knight, who was also based at Rush, caused the Customs many headaches during the 1780s and if their records are to be believed he and his gang 'terrorised' the people along the Glamorgan and Gwent coasts. The Swansea captain, William Arthur, had his days of fame or infamy, especially along the Glamorgan and Gower coasts. William Doggett and John Brown appear but briefly, because by the time of their appearance – the start of the 19th century – the days of old-time smuggling were numbered.

There is no doubt that all these smugglers, at some time or another, used the numerous islands in the Bristol Channel as their 'local' bases; the distances from Nantes, Roscoff and indeed Rush demanded some convenient storeplace and stronghold that could be easily defended. Barry Island, unlikely though it seems knowing the place today, was really an island in those times and the Connors first used it, later Thomas Knight and, after he had been cleared from there, William Doggett came for a short spell. Flat Holm was 'settled' by the Robinsons and later by others. Denny Island was used as a storehouse and, of course, Lundy Island was used as a smuggling depôt for most of the 18th century, most notably by Thomas Benson and later by Knight.

Bristol Channel itself posed a number of problems for the smugglers. First of all they had to contend with the treacherous coasts and dangerous sandbanks. The high tidal range could present difficulties for those who had little experience of its vagaries; if they were not very careful they could be left high and dry on a mud-flat – an easy prey for the Revenue forces. Unlike other smuggling coasts there were few open and sandy beaches to facilitate the landing and distribution of large cargoes, thus there were very few of the large-scale smuggling runs that were such a feature of Essex, Kent, Sussex and Dorset smuggling. Also quite strangely there were almost no

instances of outright violence, which characterised smuggling elsewhere. It would appear that the Irish smugglers were more prepared
to land their cargoes by stealth and subterfuge rather than seek or
court outright confrontation with the various Revenue forces.

However, the Bristol Channel smugglers had one distinct advantage over their counterparts in southern and eastern England, they
held an almost unchallenged command of the Channel for most of
the century and this was not really achieved by their own strength
and endeavours but rather by the Customs default. Despite con-
tinuous and insistent pleas by a number of Customs collectors there
was never more than a token presence of Revenue vessels in the
Channel and they showed even less spirited opposition. Long
stretches of the coast on both sides of the Channel were quite devoid
of Customs men, riding officers were a rarity rather than commonplace. So if the journey to the Channel was long and perilous, the
landing of goods was relatively simple and safe with the risk of
capture slender. This situation prevailed until the early years of the
19th century, when at long last Revenue cutters became very evident
and most active, preventive stations were established to guard the
danger spots and finally the Coastguard was formed with a strong
and positive force stationed along the Channel coasts.

Judged solely on the relatively few Customs and Excise seizures of
note, it would appear that smuggling in the Bristol Channel was of
little consequence and importance – a view surely held by the
Customs Head Office in London. However, it is evident from other
sources that the illegal trade flourished with conspicuous success,
albeit if not quite to the same volume and extent as in other areas.
Nevertheless the Bristol Channel has its full share of smuggling
memorabilia, as the number of 'smugglers cave and holes', brandy
coves, 'smugglers' lanes and paths' and 'smuggling inns' that
abound along its coasts show, as well as the countless smuggling
legends that still have currency. Clear of the violence and brutality
that tarnished smuggling elsewhere, the Bristol Channel smugglers
come closest to matching the romantic view of smugglers – the bold,
fearless and upright free-traders – and recalling the 'good days'
when 'a boatman might smuggle honest, didn't go astealing and
wasn't afraid to die for his principles'.

3

The Haven of Bristol

Bristol is probably the unlikeliest site for a major port in the whole of the Kingdom; not only does its entrance lie many miles up a difficult and dangerous waterway with its menacing sandbanks and daunting tides, but the port itself is situated some seven miles from the sea reached by a long and winding journey up a muddy and treacherous river. It is therefore most surprising to discover that Bristol survived as a port let alone that for many centuries it was the second largest seaport in the country. Furthermore until the meteoric rise of Liverpool in the late 18th century it was acknowledged as the gateway to the Western oceans and the New World.

The port's very situation had a considerable influence on the smuggling activities in and around Bristol. In broad terms it could be said that Bristol's contribution to the illegal trade was more of a passive than active nature. The long and tortuous journey up the Avon militated against much smuggling activity of note. If for no other reason than the vessels were captive to the river with its muddy banks and tides, their passage was slow and there was no quick and easy method of escape.

Vessels bound for the port arrived at Hungroad, near the infamous Horseshoe Bend, some four miles from the city's quays and wharves. It was at this place where the masters waited for a high tide before continuing up river through the spectacular scenery of the Avon Gorge, which surely must be the most splendid approach to any port in the world. It was at Hungroad that the Customs tidewaiters boarded the incoming vessels and stayed on board until all the cargo was discharged. They brought their own bed and 'victuals' and until the 1830s were even allowed to be accompanied by their wives! The very presence of these Customs officers had a salutary preventive effect though it must be said that they were bribed on many instances 'to look the other way'.

Unlike most great sea-ports Bristol had its quays and later docks in the heart of the city. Other major ports such as Hull, Glasgow, Liverpool, Southampton and even London had their own special dock areas generally some distance away from the city centres. This

68

has been a special feature of Bristol throughout the centuries, which makes it a unique maritime city and has excited visitors through the ages. Alexander Pope in 1732 found, 'In the middle of the streets, as far as you can see, hundred of ships, their masts as thick as they can stand by one another, which is the oddest and most surprising sight imaginable . . .'

This close proximity to the city streets made the landing and sale of smuggled goods a relatively simple and safe operation; this fact is borne out by the number of seizures of smuggled goods made in the streets and houses surrounding the quays; they were far more numerous than any other large port. During the early 19th century when large docks with formidable high walls were being constructed in other major ports, the Bristol authorities were not only slow to recognise the changes but when they constructed their docks they were open-planned, which further assisted the illegal landing of goods and caused endless problems for the Customs to control properly and adequately.

There is a smuggling axiom that for the illegal trade to flourish there must be a close and ready market for goods in quantity. The South Wales smugglers serviced the rapidly growing industrial hinterland of the valleys. Bristol provided the market for the English side of the Channel. Not only did most roads in the West Country lead to Bristol but every Channel port, however small, had a regular link by sea with Bristol. During the 18th century Bristol was a heavily industrial area with flourishing glass, paper, soap, brick and linen works besides the various trades associated with large ports – wines and spirits, tobacco, beer and ship-building. Furthermore there were several coalmines in the area, the colliers of which had long demonstrated their scant regard for all types of authority. Indeed during this period Bristol was notorious for its unruly mobs and its volatile populace. Another factor to be considered is the Bristolians' reputation for strong radical and independent views, which would suggest that they would greatly support the free-traders.

This independent attitude can be seen very early in the port's history. In 1203 King John imposed a duty of $\frac{1}{15}$th on all imports and exports (the quindecima) and provided for officials to be appointed to deal with it – 'six or seven of the wiser and more learned men of substance in the port'. When one considers the importance of Bristol then as a port it is somewhat surprising to find no record of the port in any of the duty accounts. However, on closer examination the answer is quite simple – the Bristol merchants quite adamantly refused to pay the new duty!

The merchants had previously been allowed to collect their own Customs dues and they resented the appointment of King's officials to act as collectors. They refused to appoint their 'seven wise men', continued their old practice and locked the poor and unfortunate collector in the castle keep. Two King's justices sent to investigate suffered the same fate and it took an army to restore order. The merchants' ringleaders were 'outlawed' (their property and estates forfeited to the Crown) and were not only forced to pay the full outstanding duties but were also heavily fined.

In 1387, the Collector of the 'Great Port' (there were only 13 in the Kingdom) of Bristol was ordered by the Exchequer to clear 'the Severn Sea of pyrates and divers persons who make large frauds on the King's revenue'. This is the first evidence that smuggling has a long history in the Bristol Channel. Just four years later the Collector, William Canynges, whose family later became influential merchants in the port, was told in no uncertain terms that the 'many frauds' that take place on the Western coasts should cease forthwith or else he would be made personally responsible for the revenue lost! Canynges commissioned a vessel at his own expense to cruise the coasts of his port (from Bridgwater to Chepstow) but there is no surviving evidence to show how successful this enterprise was. However, in 1429 a 'Custom House boat' was stationed at the port – the first recorded Customs vessel. It is quite likely that this vessel (which cost £22 to build) was used to carry the tide-waiters up the river to meet the incoming vessels as they arrived at the mouth of the Avon; there are certainly no records of any seizures of smuggled goods made by its crew.

By the mid 17th century the single most important commodity entering the port was tobacco, much of it was for re-export. There were continual reports of 'widespread frauds' in the trade. John Fitzgerald, the Bristol Collector, was told that he was 'to do all within his power to stamp out this pernicious trade'. Fitzgerald was in a slight dilemma because besides his official post he was also a fairly substantial merchant in the Newfoundland trade. However, he was well aware that he had to show that something was being done. In six months from May 1661 no less than ten cases of 'frauds' were reported to London – more than had been reported in the previous ten years! The majority of the cases appeared to be tobacco for export but which had been merely relanded further along the Bristol Channel. The Customs boat at Hungroad found four bales of tobacco 'hidden along the banks of the river near Bedminster'. The Customs men had great difficulty in securing the tobacco due to the 'anger and tumult of the people, who gathered in great number, who brandished scythes, forks and battens'. The Bristol merchant who was indirectly involved in this incident (he owned the offending vessel) was Rowland Trupp, who was also the Customs Customer for Bristol. A 'customer' was a very ancient patent post, whose main function was to safeguard the duty collected and to act as an independent check on the collector. It was a most profitable situation with a large income derived from fees. Thrupp remained in his post despite very strong evidence that he was deeply involved in the tobacco frauds within the port.

In 1679 a Joshua Wright, who belonged to a prominent family of merchants in the port, wrote a long letter accusing several Customs officials in Bristol of being in league with 'the fraudsters' and also for taking large bribes. He maintained that there were many illegal landings of tobacco at the mouth of the river from vessels before they came to the wharves. He asserted that many officers 'had grown rich on their ill-gotten gains'. His letter was taken seriously and two Treasury officials came down from London to investigate. They found a parlous state of affairs. They found that there was practically no Customs control, goods were landed without prior payment of duty and according to their report 'the last six tobacco shipps had not been rummaged and no exact accompt made of the goods landed'. Several officials were suspended, the two main culprits 'had escaped over the seas' and surprisingly enough Wright was appointed to one of the vacant posts – the lucrative position of land-waiter. Perhaps that had been his objective all along?

Just one year later it was reported that a party of Customs officers had attempted to seize a large quantity of smuggled goods – brandy and tobacco – which was hidden in the Forest of Arne. However, they were set upon by the local villagers and were 'opposed by riots and great violence'. Several of the officers were injured, one quite seriously and finally a troop of dragoons were called out to assist the officers and restore some order. Their arrival was slightly too late to secure the goods; they had been spirited away.

The Customs Service in Bristol appeared to be beset and bedevilled by more frauds than other ports. There were frequent internal inquiries with officers being suspended from duty but despite these frequent purges it was a most corrupt port. The largest fraud was uncovered in 1685 when the Collector, John Dutton Cole, exposed a massive collusion between the merchants and several officers. Over 22 persons were implicated and the enquiry resulted in the payment of fines in excess of £2,700. Several of the guilty officers were placed in the public pillory and no doubt suffered at the hands of their fellow citizens!

A group of merchants attempted to get their own back on Cole by implicating him in another fraud. It was a well-planned 'set-up' with forged letters and receipts as well as perjured evidence. Cole managed to survive a full Treasury inquiry and prove his innocence and he lasted in post until 1700. Though two years after his retirement it came to light that he owed the Crown no less than £3,000 in unremitted duties. He was allowed to pay the money back over two years though it does cast a shadow on his innocence!

One of Cole's more successful coups was to discover that two Bristol merchants who regularly supplied tobacco to France and claimed the duty refund, were actually 'exporting' it merely across the Bristol Channel to Chepstow. The goods were landed at the mouth of the river Wye. Cole maintained that much of the tobacco came back to Bristol via the many market boats that regularly plied across the Channel. The merchants were heavily fined (£1,000 each), they lost the tobacco (over 13,000 pounds in weight) and were very fortunate not to end up in prison, especially as Cole averred that they had been operating this fraud for the last two years at least.

The treacherous nature of the Bristol Channel can be seen in a most tragic accident that occurred in March 1705 when no less than 20 Customs tidesmen and boatmen were drowned at the mouth of the river Avon in what was described as 'a most calamatous and fierce storm'. These men represented nearly a third of the total Customs staff at the port and as such it must have been a tragedy of some magnitude. Each widow received an annual pension of £7-10s and £1-10s for each child. One sad case cites 'a motherless daughter aged eight years', who was considered 'a widow for pension purposes'.

It was to be another two years before two new boats were provided for the port and the Collector made it quite clear to London that he could not be held responsible for goods being 'runned on these shores if you cannot supply a sturdy boat or boats that was strongly armed.' This was at a time when the port was entering its richest era. The American and West Indian trade was increasing rapidly and almost half that of London. The import of sugar had become a major factor in the port and the Bristol merchants were preparing to enter the very lucrative slave trade. During this period little is heard of any frauds in the port or indeed of any smuggling.

In 1700 the *Anna*, a vessel bound from Barbados to Cork (via Bristol) was cleared for sailing – in effect the Customs ensured that no prohibited goods were being exported. However, they found that one of the sailors had 'ten yards of flannel to make himself apparel'.

This was seized and he was removed to gaol. Then (and for the rest of the century) the exportation of wool was strictly prohibited.

The Excise officers in the city were not idle and there were several seizures of tobacco and spirits from shops and houses in the myriad of streets and alleys that backed onto the wharves. One incident is particularly amusing, an Excise officer happened to miss his footing and he fell headlong into the cellar of an inn in Bridge Street. When he had recovered from his fall he decided to inspect the premises and found a quantity of brandy, rum and some bottles of sack that were not 'permitted' (all movements of duty-paid spirits and wine required an Excise permit as evidence of duty payment). The innkeeper, who rejoiced under the name of Boaz Pritchard (there was always a large Welsh colony in Bristol) argued rather in vain that the officer had no right to search his cellars. In this he was quite wrong. Excise officers had the right of entry and search to any premises where Exciseable goods were either produced or stored. Pritchard was heavily fined and the seized goods were put up for auction.

It was in 1717 that the Collector first petitioned for a smack to be provided to guard against smugglers 'landing goods on the creeks and obscure places of this port'. This plea would be repeated countless times by the Bristol Collector and echoed by other Channel collectors throughout the rest of the century. He added that his officers had received information that goods were regularly being run on the Somerset coast right from Portishead to Uphill near Weston-super-Mare. He pointed out that he could get a vessel built for £120, which would cost £80 per annum to keep and this expenditure would be amply compensated by the value of the extra seizures. However, his appeal fell on deaf ears.

As if to justify this view, just 18 months later, the Bridgwater Collector reported to the Board in London that a Hamburgh vessel had gone ashore near the limits of his port and Bristol (possibly Brean Down or Burnham). It would appear that 370 casks of wine, 96 casks of brandy as well as a quantity of other goods were salvaged and placed under Customs seals. The master of the vessel had no money to pay the salvage claims and his agent in Bristol applied for permission to sell a portion of the cargo or to send them by sea to Bristol. However, the local 'smugglers' broke into the Customs cellars and helped themselves to some of the wine and brandy. The Board in London offered a reward for their capture and both collectors were told to use their utmost efforts to apprehend the offenders.

The Bristol agent wrote to Earle, the local M.P. and asked him to   73 use his influence to get troops sent to the area, '50 or 60 men carried off 6 casks of brandy and many bottles of wine ... The Customs would have searched for it but 40 or 50 villaines with Forks, Shovels etc opposed them, Swearing Bitterly they would murder every soul of 'em ... we cannot leave them [the crew] to be Devoured by Beares'. The London Board recommended that a troop of soldiers be sent from Bristol forthwith. Unfortunately the outcome of the incident is not known as the final papers have gone missing. It is interesting to note that it was not until 1776 that it was enacted that when wrecks are plundered, a penalty would be imposed on the hundred where the wreck occurred, though it must be said that this enactment had little practical effect on the wrecking habits of the West Country people.

Some two years after this outbreak of violence the Bristol collector addressed a strong letter to London about a 'recent smuggling Act'. Although he thought that it was 'admirable in theory' it was of no practical use unless he was provided with sufficient officers to oppose the smugglers. He further pointed out that within the whole of his port there were only four firearms, one was so rusty that it did not operate and the other three had been in the Custom House for 15 years. One must remember that Bristol was then the second largest port in the country, such was the unpreparedness of the Customs Service to meet the sudden and rapid increase in smuggling. The Act, the Collector was referring to, was passed in 1719 and it legislated that smugglers assembling to a number of eight or more and 'hindering, beating or wounding officers' should be transported to the Plantations and by 1721 the number was reduced to five. Like many of the later smuggling Acts it was hardly ever used for the simple fact that the Customs officers could hardly ever gather in sufficient numbers to oppose groups of smugglers in force.

The increased violence of the smugglers was clearly shown in 1725 when a gang was discovered unloading brandy and tobacco near Portishead Point. The Customs vessel, probably no more than a large rowing boat with a single sail, which had come inshore to seize the goods was soundly beaten off by the smugglers, all of whom were 'heavily armed'. The Customs men were powerless to intervene and were forced to watch, at a safe distance, the landing and subsequent escape of the 'smuggling wherry'. By the time the Customs men had landed to search for the goods, they had long since disappeared. Perhaps as a result of this blatent and insolent act, a Naval vessel *Fame* was ordered to patrol the Channel from the Avon to Hartland Point. There is no evidence that the vessel made any substantial seizures and in less than twelve months it was removed to other duties.

It is very unlikely that the Navy men received much assistance or information from the Customs. At this time the Customs probably detested the Navy more than they did the smugglers. They took great pleasure in interfering with the Navy's operations as much as possible. Naval ships arriving from foreign ports were arrested and placed in quarantine, the movement of stores was frustrated and the Customs officers took great delight in rummaging Naval vessels. In some part the Customs officers were demonstrating the country's anti-militarism but this was heightened by the knowledge that most Naval men were themselves inveterate smugglers and furthermore a fair percentage of the crew were convicted smugglers, who since 1704 had been released from prison sentences provided they joined the Navy.

The Excise officers in Bristol also suffered at the hands of the smugglers. In 1738 it was reported that 'the unruly colliers in Kingswood' were not only selling ale and cider that they had illegally produced but they were at the centre of the smuggling of brandy and rum. This 'strange crew', as the Excise supervisor called them, numbered in excess of 1,000 and all attempts to collect the Excise duty on the ale and cider had been resisted with utmost force and with the use of firearms. Eventually the Army was called out to support the Excise officers and a full-scale military operation ensued. However, the problem was never really resolved as there were almost continual reports of 'outrages' later on in the century and they, in part, made up Bristol's volatile crowds causing trouble well into the following century. Indeed during the famous or infamous Reform Bill riots of 1831 they played a leading part. It was during these riots that both the Custom House and the Excise Office were destroyed by fire.

An interesting insight into a more sedate type of smuggling is highlighted in 1735 when the Collector reported that 'there were a number of women of fashion entering the port', so much so that the Collector had felt it neccesary to employ the wife of one of the tide-waiters to act as 'a female searcher'. He was probably referring to the number of women passengers returning from the American and West Indian colonies. The Customs Board were already alive to the situation and had previously issued a general letter to all the ports suggesting that 'women passengers carry customable goods about their person' and that a female should be employed in whom 'they could confide'!

Almost as some justification of this action the Excise seized 'a large quantity of silk and silk goods' as it was being loaded onto a   75

The Clifton Suspension Bridge – surely the most splendid approach to any port in the world.

carriage at an inn in the city. The baggage belonged to the wife and daughters of a West Indian sugar planter, who had an estate near Bath. The baggage had already been cleared by the Customs. The incident caused quite a storm between the two Services with petitions and cross-petitions flying back and forth to London. Ultimately the Treasury had to intervene. The seizure of the goods was not maintained but released on payment of the duty and certainly no fine was imposed on the ladies. One could say that there was one law for the rich and one for the poor. Or perhaps it was more a case of having friends in high places!

The other side of the coin is vividly illustrated by the sad case of Thomas Body, who in 1760, was languishing in Bristol Gaol. He petitioned the Collector for his release on the grounds that he was the sole support of his mother and three sisters. Body had been convicted of smuggling just over one pound of tobacco and had been imprisoned because he could not pay the fine. Body claimed to be only 13 years old but the Customs doubted this, 'his worldliness and knowledge are such that we consider him to be at least 16 years old'! Again the vital papers are missing so it is not known whether his petition was successful, but unless he was able to obtain the support of some person of substance he would have been unlikely to have been released.

In 1755 the Customs Board in London received an anonymous sum of £30 from 'a merchant of Bristol' – most probably 'conscience money' for a past misdeed. One wonders whether this merchant was a newly converted Methodist – the Wesley brothers had long been associated with Bristol. John Wesley was one of the few prominent public figures not prepared to condone smuggling. During his preaching tours he constantly exhorted against 'the accursed thing, smuggling'. His hatred of the trade led him to refrain from drinking tea as the majority of this commodity was smuggled. Wesley considered 'every smuggler is a thief general, who picks the pockets, both of the King and all his fellow subjects. He wrongs them all.'

The Bristol Channel pilots were a constant problem to not only the Bristol officers but to all the Customs along the Channel. They had a universal reputation as being smugglers par excellence and indeed few were ever caught at the trade. They had the best opportunity, they met incoming vessels at Lundy Island or frequently far beyond into the Western approaches. Their seamanship and knowledge of the Channel waters was without equal. And although they were in keen and cut-throat opposition with each other, they lived in a tight, secure and secretive community without the threat of informers.

Pill, a small village on the banks of the Avon, was for several centuries the home of these intrepid mariners. It had long been a creek of the port of Bristol – in other words it was of sufficient importance to warrant the presence of a Customs officer. The first known Customs watch-house at Pill was built in 1693 (though there might have been an earlier building). The watch-house was re-built in 1850 and it still survives, though now in private occupation. Few pilots were ever convicted of smuggling, some of the 'westermen' were fined for minor smuggling. The 'westermen' were the mariners (usually a man and a boy) who brought the cutter back to Pill after the pilot had boarded an incoming vessel.

Every so often the Bristol officers would make a promiscuous search of the village and the cutters lying at the mud berths of the creek. In each of these forays the Customs men made a number of small seizures of tobacco or tea and the odd bottle of wine. However, it seems as if these small parcels of goods were left to be found in order to justify the search and to keep the authorities fairly happy with the situation – a grand cat and mouse game!

However, in 1763, Richard Neale – the officer at Pill – received some information about goods being regularly landed near Portbury. I take this to mean the stretch of coast where Avonmouth or the Royal

77

A cartoon of King William IV in the uniform of the Preventive Service.

Portbury Docks are now sited. The Collector took this information seriously and detailed a party of officers to watch the coast. They spent an abortive three days and three nights at the spot without any movement and they finally decided to leave. Some two weeks later the Collector heard that a large quantity of brandy and tobacco had been landed in the area from the *Eleanor Warren* a vessel bound from the West Indies. The vessel was still in the port and it received a special rummage by the Customs. They found 'Bottles of wine and sack' hidden under ropes and sails. The master vehemently protested his innocence and stated that the goods were for 'smuggling into the Indies'! Nevertheless they were seized and were subsequently found to have come from an Excise warehouse in the port.

The Excise had a little better success against the Channel pilots. One pilot, James Hall, was apprehended by an Excise officer in Easton-in-Gordano, near Pill because he was carrying a suspicious package. After a certain amount of argument as to whether the Excise officer had the right to see what was in the parcel, Hall was forced to disclose its contents – several small packages of tea totalling less than five pounds in weight. Hall was fined £2, which would have been of little consequence to him as the Channel pilots received more than that for piloting a vessel from Lundy. Incidentally they received their fee even if the master refused their services – pilotage from Lundy was compulsory. A report on Hall was passed to the Society of Merchants at Bristol who controlled the pilots but no further action was taken against Hall.

Some three years later, in 1763, the Excise cutter *Lawton*, which was based at Swansea for a period, sighted a pilot cutter acting suspiciously off Bull Point near Ilfracombe. Ignoring the signals to hove-to it set off up the Channel and the *Lawton* gave chase. The Channel pilot should have been odds-on favourite to escape but he was opposed by a most determined commander – John Pickering. Despite the pilot's better knowledge of the Channel waters and a slightly faster vessel he was slowly being over-hauled. The pilot decided to off-load several ankers of brandy, this was a frequently used ruse to evade capture, cutter commanders were under strict orders to recover and secure such goods and the time spent on this operation invariably allowed the smuggling vessel time to escape. Not this time though for Pickering ignored the casks and finally overhauled the cutter near Kingroad (at the mouth of the Avon). Four bales of tobacco and some packages of tea were found on board. The pilot (his name does not appear in the report) was heavily fined and indeed was very fortunate not to have his vessel seized.

Although it is very true to say that the majority of goods smuggled in the Bristol Channel were tobacco, brandy, rum and wines; it is quite clear that any commodity which would show a reasonable profit was likely to be smuggled. During the 1760/1770s such diverse articles as vinegar, starch, soap, candles and sail-cloth were seized at Bristol. Six casks of vinegar were taken off the Spanish vessel *Phillipe y Maria* in 1764. The goods were not hidden as such but rather had not been reported to the Customs. It is surely no coincidence that only twelve months earlier an additional Customs duty had been placed on foreign vinegar, which made it almost as costly as wine.

During this period there were a number of small seizures of starch mainly from the numerous cross-Channel market boats that berthed at or near the Welsh Back. This would seem to suggest that the starch was smuggled out of Ireland and either landed at one of the small Channel ports where the Customs presence was slight or been transferred at sea. It was quite difficult to distinguish starch from flour, a point recognised by the Customs Board and so they issued special instructions to their staff:

'Put it in a tumbler of water, which if Starch will sink to the Bottom and form a hard substance, and if Flour will then turn into Paste and may be drawn into a kind of string like doe [dough] and further by Starch being much whiter than flour'

In theory illegal imports of sail-cloth should have been far easier to discover if only on account of its bulk. Since 1713 there had been an import duty on sail-cloth and duty-paid cloth was stamped by the Customs using large wooden stamps to mark the cloth (these stamps were often two feet square and had the name of the port marked, several have survived). In 1748 Irish sail-cloth was made dutiable and suddenly all English vessels arriving from Ireland with such sails had to pay duty, which was quite considerable. During the next ten years there were several seizures of sails from the many vessels arriving from Ireland. Quite a number of ruses were tried to avoid the duty – even forged 'duty-paid' stamps – but most seizures were made from the sail-cloth either being hidden in the cargo or concealed with old sails. There was one clever concealment that certainly deserves a mention. It was discovered on the *Catherine Lacey* from Cork. The new sails had been carefully secured to the sides of the vessel well below the waterline so that they were not visible either from the deck or from the quay. However, as the cargo was discharged the vessel lightened and rose higher out of the water and thus revealed the sail-cloth. It does seem rather strange that after all the trouble the master had taken to hide the sails he should have forgotten such an obvious fact!

Because of the extensive smuggling of candles, soap and starch, the legal minimum size for imports was raised to 224 pounds. By this stroke of a legal pen any small quantities of such goods found on board, whether they were hidden or not, became liable to seizure. Perhaps a somewhat inequitable measure but similar restrictions applied to tobacco, tea and spirits. At least such enactments did wonders for the seizure records of the port!

Help for the beleaguered Customs staff also came in a different form – the information the Collector received from London was frequent and quite detailed in content. For example in 1775 he was notified that there were four vessels from Cardigan, each loading salt in Ireland and it was stated that it was their intention to land it illegally on the Bristol Channel coasts – what was missing was the precise location. Just one month later another letter arrived from London informing him that the *Elizabeth Jane* from Holland was bound for Ireland with a cargo of spirits and tobacco concealed in a false bottom; furthermore it was believed that the goods were destined to be landed somewhere in the Bristol Channel. And yet again, barely two months later, further information was supplied about a vessel from the Channel Islands with a cargo of tea, spirits, and 'French goods' was due in the Bristol Channel 'within the next two weeks'. Unfortunately there is no evidence to show that any of this information resulted in any seizures.

It was very clear that the London Board had set up a good channel of information from abroad and indeed their network of informers improved over the next 30 or so years. But it did prove to be quite expensive. They paid a certain Emmanuel Mathias no less than £312-18s-8d for 'expenses incurred on gathering information on the Continent.' According to a note in the margin of the account Mathias was 'a merchant of Bristol and known to the Collector at that port' – almost as if that was some sort of approval for such a large payment. The Collector at the time was Daniel Harson, who had previously been a dissenting minister and had obtained his plum post by marrying the previous Collector's daughter! Harson was not a particularly successful or popular official. He managed to antagonise his staff and the merchants alike and he caused considerable friction with the port's trading community. Probably as a result of the merchant's complaints to the Treasury, the Customs Board found it necessary to order Harson and his staff 'to behave soberly, civilly and with good manners towards each other as well as to the merchants.'

81

The American Revolution or 'Rebellion' as it was known then, caused considerable extra work for the Bristol officers. Vessels bound for the West Indian or American colonies were 'to be rummaged very closely and any letters going to persons in the provinces actually in rebellion' were to be detained. Also persons arriving from America were required to be strictly examined and their letters and papers sent directly to London. Even after the Republic had been declared, some of the Bristol officers refused to clear a French vessel which had goods for the United States. They were informed by no less a body than the Privy Council that foreign vessels may now trade with the newly recognised American Republic, hitherto they had been forbidden to trade under the old Navigation Acts.

During the 1780s the pattern of smuggling in the port did not greatly change. There were a considerable number of small seizures of tobacco and spirits and they appeared to be made from the regular trading vessels to Bristol from the other Channel ports. Two Spanish sailors were caught 'hawking their wares around the streets'. It would seem that they were trying to sell some bottles of wine and brandy. Their defence, put forward by a Bristol merchant (the Spanish Consul?), was that they were so poorly paid and had large families to support that they had little alternative than to indulge in 'some venturing'. Nobody was impressed by this excuse and both men were dragged off to serve in the Navy. An Excise officer found 25 pounds of tea 'secreted under wood shavings in a timber yard off Queen's Square'. Considering that this was virtually within sight of both the Custom House and the Excise Office, one gains the impression that it was not too difficult to land goods from vessels whilst they were in port. The Collector, John Powell, was forced to admit to an Inspector from London that 'this port is the most open in the Kingdom and even given twice the officers it would still be difficult to stop the trade.' Powell was a hard taskmaster, who tried to instil some urgency into his officers, perhaps his previous experience as 'a medical man on a slave ship' had some bearing on this.

There was only one seizure of note during the decade. In May 1787 an Irish vessel *Jeanne* arrived from Dublin with a cargo of foodstuffs and cattle. It was rummaged by the Customs on arrival, who found nothing untoward. Then three days later they returned and searched the vessel (perhaps they were acting on information?), this time they discovered a rather clever concealment between the bitts and stern. The entrance to this space was carefully 'tarred and let into the planking'. It was less than half full but still contained sixteen small bales of tobacco and six casks of rum. The master was

'On the look-out' was a familiar smuggling expression.

Michael Barry, who claimed to be a Frenchman and that his 'proper' name was Dubarry. Indeed he produced papers that showed that he resided at Lorient. The Customs Solicitor advised against prosecution on the grounds that the Smuggling Acts did not cover foreigners and that it would be long and time-consuming to prove that Barry or Dubarry was not what he said. So he escaped without a penalty to carry on his smuggling trade. It is interesting to note that Barry did not carry a passport. During the 1780s passports were introduced, each one signed by the Secretary of State and indeed by 1798 no foreigner was allowed to leave the country without producing a passport, which had to be signed by the Collector before the person was allowed to embark.

Such was the state of smuggling in 1782 that the Customs Board issued a strong letter to all collectors. It is worth recording in full:

> Custom House,
> London.
> 5th January 1782

'The enormous Increase of Smuggling, the Outrages which it is carried on, the Mischiefs it Occasions to the Country, the Discouragement it Creates to all fair Traders and the Prodigious Loss the Revenue Sustains by it. We are desirous to give a Great Cheque to this National Evil but are much dismayed by our officers want of success in making captures, this Defect would not have been so if the Instructions and Orders given by this Board had been duly observed. We therefore enjoin you to carefully peruse these Orders and ensure that the officers apprehend their contents unless they ignore them at their peril'.

There is no evidence that this exhortation had any material effect on the number of seizures! Perhaps one might comment that smuggling looked vastly different from the comfort and safety of a seat in the London Custom House compared with facing the fury and violence of the smugglers on a lonely clifftop or beach in the dead of the night. Considering the meagre pensions paid by the Customs Boards to widows and to officers seriously injured in line of duty, it is not really surprising that the majority of officers decided that caution and circumspection were the best courses of action. However, the Board members and their officials – all of whom had obtained their positions by patronage – viewed the officers' actions or lack of it smacked of cowardice! Nevertheless there were many brave officers who operated against quite overwhelming odds and often suffered grievously for their dedication to duty.

Bristol, in any case, had never been in the forefront of 'seizing ports'. The principal ones, in order, were London, Yarmouth, Harwich, Dover, Sandwich, Southampton, Cowes, Plymouth and St

Ives. Towards the end of the century the port's trade was suffering badly, due to the strong competition of both Glasgow and Liverpool and Wilberforce's campaign against the slave trade. The Collector remarked, in 1796, that the number of vessels using the port had decreased by over one quarter and that tobacco imports had slumped dramatically. It was quite clear that the palmy days of the port had disappeared and during the next century its trade would fall even further. By 1800 the Customs staff at the port numbered less than thirty with a waiter at Portishead and one at Uphill – a reduction of well over 50%.

As the century drew to a close there was a last flurry of seizures. In 1798 no less than twenty ankers of brandy and rum were found hidden along the banks of the Avon near Hungroad. The Customs boat at Pill had discovered the goods by 'creeping' (that is by dragging or sounding for sunken goods or searching holes and gullies along the shore). Of course there was no way of discovering where the goods had come from or indeed who were the owners. In the same year the Customs boarded the *Rodney* from Newport loaded with coal. The boatmen found several bales of tobacco and two casks of spirits under the cargo. William Jones, the master, was forced to admit that he had obtained the goods from 'an American vessel near Flat Holm'.

It is not known whether the *Rodney* was seized and condemned. However, the Collector was reminded by London as to the regulations for breaking-up condemned vessels. It would appear that such condemned vessels were being sold and 'old and worn vessels' destroyed in their place. The instructions were clear. 'The ballast, masts, pumps and bulk-heads were to be taken out, the decks stripped and ripped fore and aft, the beams cut asunder, the bottom planks ripped off, the keels cut into four pieces and the stern posts into three'. Rowing boats that were condemned were to be cut through the thwarts, the hulls sawn into four parts and the stems and sterns cut into two. Quite a comprehensive job if the instructions were followed to the letter of the law!

It falls to the Excise to have the final word on smuggling in Bristol. It was in November 1799 late in the evening when two Excise officers were walking along St Thomas Street in the Redcliffe district of the port when they noticed a hand-cart being pushed along the street towards them. It was heavily loaded but its contents was covered by sacking. The officers moved to approach the two men who were pushing the cart and challenged them to produce their Excise permit (though in fact the movement of dutiable goods was strictly prohibited during the hours of darkness – for obvious reasons). According to the report the men did not stop and though

85

chase was given they managed to disappear amongst the numerous alleys. The cart contained four half bales of tobacco, two packages of tea and three small casks of rum. Needless to add it was never discovered where the goods had come from. Indeed very little effort was made by the authorities – long experience had taught them it was a wasteful experience.

Smugglers Attacked. A popular 19th century print by an unknown artist. (Reproduced by kind permission of Alan Hay)

It is interesting to note that there were two Excise officers at this seizure. Perhaps they had taken to patrolling in pairs for safety especially in the Redcliffe district, which had for long been a quite notorious area. Joined to the rest of the city by Bristol bridge, the place teemed with workshops, warehouses and inns and was an ideal spot for the sale and distribution of smuggled goods. Few of the old inns remain but the Ostrich in Guinea Street, built in the mid 18th century, is reputed to have been involved in the smuggling activities of the port. There is an entrance to a cave at the rear of the inn, which might have given access to the labyrinth of caves in Redcliffe Hill. These caves were quarried for the sandstone which was used in the glassworks and they were also doubled as a storehouse of smuggled goods.

The Excise seizure is a fitting end to this chapter on Bristol's smuggling past as it epitomised the nature of the illegal trade in the port. Smuggled goods being trundled through the streets almost as if the Customs and Excise authorities did not exist – a truculent show of independence almost bordering on insolence. One must wonder that if the port had been situated on the other Channel with far greater opportunities to smuggle, I am sure its citizens and mariners would have revelled in the smuggling trade.

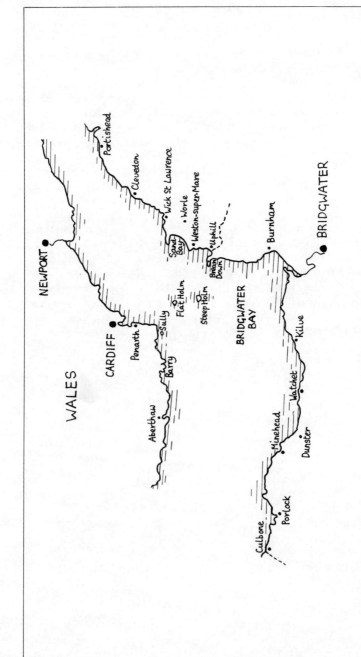

THE AVON AND SOMERSET COASTS

4

The Avon and Somerset Coasts

Until recent times it would have been quite sufficient and very correct to define the coastline that lies between the mouth of the river Avon in the north to Porlock in the south-west, as the 'Somerset shore'. Certainly all the mariners, and smugglers for that matter, would have known and recognised it as such. However, during the early 1970s it was decided to revamp all the county boundaries and as a result a new county was artificially fashioned out of a part of Somerset. The County of Avon came into being on All Fool's Day, 1974; many living in the area affected by this administrative change would no doubt subscribe to the view that the day chosen was most appropriate! Therefore it is necessary to consider the two coasts separately though few visitors to the area are aware just where the county boundary is sited. It is strange to relate that the two coasts are quite different, certainly as far as smuggling was concerned.

Although the Avon coast runs north of the river Avon, the part of the coast that concerns us stretches from Portishead in the north-east to Uphill, which is almost in a due southerly direction. The name of this coast may have been changed by bureaucrats but the landscape has remained unaltered, except that in certain places it has become very developed. The coastline can be very neatly summed up as 'cliffs and moors' – not strictly accurate but a reasonably fair description. From the bleak marshland around the mouth of the Avon, now sadly disfigured by much industrial development and the Royal Portbury Docks complex, right down to Uphill, now a respectable suburb of Weston-super-Mare, the Avon coast comprises long stretches of thick, oozy brown mud, broken up in places by several cliff ridges of not very majestic proportions – at least compared with those further down the Channel. The only extensive sandy beaches are to be found around Weston-super-Mare, one of the main reasons for its development as a seaside resort.

The topography and nature of any coastline had a very marked bearing on the activities of the smuggling fraternity; the dangers and perils the smugglers faced coming up the Bristol Channel were sufficient without adding extra problems of landing the goods on dangerous and difficult coasts. Thus it is not surprising to discover that there is little smuggling tradition or activity around the Portishead and Clevedon area, because here the long hill ridge presents a steep cliff face to the sea, with virtually no convenient or safe landing places. Furthermore this area had long suffered from its close proximity to Bristol. It is no coincidence that from the early 16th century the Customs limits of the Port of Bristol extended from Aust to Uphill, which is virtually the boundary of the present Avon coast. Within these port limits there was no other port with any substantial legal trade to help foster smuggling – the plain fact was that all sea-routes led to Bristol.

For most of the 18th and 19th centuries Portishead was merely a 'creek' in Customs parlance – a minor port deserving the attendance of a tide-waiter, a very lowly Customs officer. This is indeed quite surprising because as early as 1364 the very first Customs officials were appointed to the port. There were no less than four and they were instructed '. . . in the Port and town of Pratteshyde to make diligent scrutiny in the Port and town that none cross the sea from the realm without Royal licence and not taking gold or silver in mass, jewels or letters of exchange on pain of arrest . . .' Their greatest problem appeared to be the security of wrecked goods. There are frequent references in the State Papers of goods from wrecked vessels being washed up on the shore and rapidly disappearing before they could make them secure.

In the early years of the 17th century there were a few isolated reports of 'divers frauds with the vessels that do anchor at Kyng's Rode'. For centuries Kingroad, a sheltered haven beneath Portishead Point, had been the place of departure for vessels out of Bristol. In the days of sail the number of ships waiting a fair wind or inward vessels waiting on the tide were quite numerous. However, with the advent of steam there was little need for delay and Kingroad slowly ceased to be used as an anchorage in favour of Walton Bay further down the coast. It should also be remembered that the area around the mouth of the Avon was always well patrolled by the Customs and latterly a Revenue cutter was based there, its mere presence acting as a deterrent.

Throughout the heyday of smuggling, Portishead was not much more than a small fishing port with just a few market boats trading grain and cider to Bristol. The sea dock that so revitalised the fortunes of this ancient port was opened in 1879. However, there was a small coal wharf near the mouth of the Pill where during the 18th century coal was exported from the nearby Clapton mines, this coal went to South Wales of all places! Later the process was reversed and when the power station was built (a famous Channel landmark) a large number of coal vessels from Wales traded to the port.

In 1740 the Customs Board in London received a report from the Bristol Collector that some of his officers had 'completed a sweep of the town of Portishead and the surrounding countryside'. It was clear that they were acting on information that the vessels at anchor at Kingroad 'land goods to the detriment of the King's Revenue'. The result of the exercise was the seizure of ten barrels of wine, six bales of tobacco and a quantity of sugar. The collector was told that a greater vigilance should be maintained over the 'officers of the Waterguard'. It was another ten years before a further seizure was made, a small gig from a French vessel was taken 'on the marshland' (possibly near Severn Beach), a quantity of brandy, tobacco and liquorice (of all things!) was seized but the two Frenchmen were returned to their ship. In those days foreign nationals could not be convicted of smuggling.

The Excise were quite active in the area, especially in the Gordano valley, the flat-bottomed valley which now includes the Weston Moor Nature Reserve. In 1755 John Lane, an Excise officer, stopped a suspicious farm cart and was set upon by 'several ruffians' near Weston-in-Gordano. For his pains he was left with cuts, bruises and a sore head and just two kegs of brandy, the miscreants having made their escape. Several years later an Excise supervisor reported to his collector in Bristol that the valley people were 'very prone to the illegal trade', however there was no hard evidence or further seizures to prove or disprove this opinion. According to a local historian most of the older houses in the valley had capacious cellars dug out of the earth, which were most likely used to conceal smuggled goods. In 1786 an Excise officer found 'six bags of salt in a cellar of an inn in Weston'. The inn-keeper stoutly maintained that the salt was duty-paid but he could not produce the evidence nor indeed explain why he had such a quantity. The officer seized the salt as he considered it to be of 'Irish origin because of the size of the grains' – an interesting comment.

During the 1770s there was a battle raging between the Collector at Cardiff and his counterpart across the Channel at Bristol. The Cardiff Collector had regularly complained about the goods that were being smuggled on 'the colliers', he appeared to be referring to the vessels from Portishead. In desperation he complained to London and as a direct result several small seizures of tobacco, spirits and wine were made by the Bristol officers at Portishead. Of course within 20 years the boot was on the other foot when Cardiff, Newport and Aberthaw became coal-exporting ports. In 1810 a Preventive Waterguard station was established at Portishead; their watch-house was sited on the edge of the pill below Woodhill and the building only disappeared at the end of the 19th century. Indeed little more is heard of smuggling in the area though it still probably continued in a minor way.

There is a legend in the area that during the latter decades of the 18th century several smugglers were executed at Bristol and then hung in chains on Dunball Island at the mouth of the Avon – possibly as a warning to the crews of the many vessels that passed the island on route to and from Bristol. Although it is known that several murderers suffered this fate there is no evidence to support the story. Actually, throughout the 18th century relatively few smugglers were executed for their crimes, largely because few juries were prepared to convict them; some were transported but by far the majority were impressed into the Navy and proved themselves to be excellent seamen.

Female smugglers specialized in concealing dutiable goods under their clothing, often disguising illicit cargoes of lace, silk and even soap as advanced pregnancy.

Just along the coast is Clevedon, never more than a handful of cottages around a church situated above a rocky bay, until it became a rather superior seaside resort in the 1840s. It is famed now for its splendid Victorian pier and its literary connections with Tennyson and Hallam. The Hallams' country seat was Clevedon Court and Arthur Hallam is buried in the church 'on the hill' – '. . . They laid him by the pleasant shore. And in the hearing of the wave . . .' There appear to be no smuggling incidents in the area even though one can walk from Portishead to Clevedon by way of a cliff-top path, known as the Coastguard way, which at least demonstrates that this part of the coast warranted some Revenue presence.

The marshland south of Clevedon, with its long stretches of chocolate mud, was never really conducive to the illegal landing of goods. The navigational hazards of this part of the coast were notorious; the 'Clevedon Flats' were specially noted in a late 18th century chart as 'very treacherous channels'. In 1838 the famous lightship, the *English and Welsh Grounds* was established six miles off Clevedon marking the dangerous sands. It could claim to be the most hazardous stretch of water in the whole of the Bristol Channel. Therefore it is perhaps not surprising that there are no smuggling legends in the area. It could be, of course, that no Revenue vessel dared to cruise in the area and therefore the smugglers had a clear field. However, one must point out that the moorlands would have posed almost insuperable problems in transporting goods away from the shore.

From the dykes and rynes of the estuary of the river Yeo, the land rises rather majestically to Middle Hope, cliffs of somewhat minor proportions but which nevertheless afford splendid views up and down the coast and across the Channel to the Welsh coast. The area is still not very accessible despite its closeness to Weston-super-Mare, so during the days of smuggling it was quite remote. It is at present in the hands of the National Trust. Woodspring Bay (originally Worspring) is noted mainly for the ruins of an early 13th century priory, owned by Landmark Trust (who are also responsible for Lundy Island). But less well-known is the Bay's smuggling reputation.

As early as 1689 'the creek of Worspring' was shown in the 'Port of Bristow'; however, much of its trade was smuggling. It was (or indeed is) a perfect site for smuggling: a sandy bay beneath cliffs, which gave a rare vantage point both to land and to sea. It also had the advantages of small caves and being well away from any roads; the nearest Revenue officer was stationed at Uphill some seven or eight difficult miles away. Even when the Preventive Waterguard

Custom-House, London,

Notice is hereby Given,

THAT from and after the 5th day of January, 1826, all Vessels not square rigged, and all Boats except Whale Boats, Boats employed in the Fisheries, Boats belonging to square rigged Vessels in the Merchants' Service, Tow Boats used in towing Vessels belonging to licenced Pilots, and Boats used solely in Rivers and Inland Navigation, will in pursuance of the Act of the 6th Geo. IV. ch. 108, be subject to seizure and forfeiture, unless the Owners thereof shall have obtained a Licence for navigating the same, from the Commissioners of His Majesty's Customs.

This Notice is therefore given by the said Commissioners, in order that the Owners of all Vessels and Boats, requiring Licences under the above Act, may forthwith make application to the proper Officers of the Customs at the Port to which such Vessels and Boats belong, and take the necessary measures for procuring Licences for the same, prior to the 5th January, 1826.

By Order of the Commissioners,

T. WHITMORE,
Secretary.

Teape, Printer, Tower-hill, London

One of the measures used to control smuggling vessels.

was established in 1810 the officers were based at Weston near Birn Beck Island, still a good distance from the Bay. Perhaps it is not too surprising that few seizures were made there. In the whole of the 18th century there are only two recorded incidents. In 1783 an Excise officer seized 'ten tubs of brandy hidden in the woods near Kew Stoke'. Four years later John Huish, tide-waiter at Uphill, along with a group of militia arrived at the Bay just as smuggled goods were being loaded onto horses. After 'a desperate affray' most of the goods (20 bales of tobacco, 40 ankers of spirits and 'other packages') were secured but apparently all the smugglers made their escape. Huish must have been acting on information, otherwise he would not have been able to call on the assistance of the military. It is not really surprising that no smugglers were apprehended in this instance because most of the militia were in sympathy with the smugglers and in any case their reward money for the night's work would have been calculated purely on the value of the goods seized.

Such was the reputation of the area that in the early 1830s an old Revenue cutter, the *Diligence*, which had seen long service in various Devon and Cornish ports, was towed to the estuary of the Yeo and beached and became a Coastguard station with a complement of one officer and five men. Indeed one of the last large smuggling runs in the Bristol Channel took place here in 1845 when 250 barrels of spirits were landed in the Bay. The Coastguardmen managed to recover most of the goods but as the local newspaper recorded, 'the parties having evaded the vigilance of the Coastguard'! There was no doubt that 'heads would roll' as a result of this incident. At this time there was a Coastguard order which stated that any men servir.g at a station where a successful run of smuggled goods had taken place would not be considered for promotion or 'any mark of indulgence or favour'.

In 1825 – several years before the Coastguard station was established at the Bay – a Revenue cutter based at Ilfracombe named the *Harpy* was cruising on patrol when it discovered a small fishing smack anchored just inside the Bay. On making a routine check the Revenue men found that the fishermen had been landing some ankers of brandy, but all except one cask had been landed. The Commander sent a party ashore to search for the goods and maybe to apprehend the smugglers. The men returned empty handed, both goods and men had disappeared without a trace. The fishing smack was brought back to Ilfracombe and subsequently condemned as Crown property. It received the same fate as all seized smuggling vessels (at least those which were not considered of use to the Customs), it was sawn into three parts. The collector in his report to London made little of the incident, he was no doubt aware that the cutter was outside its allotted patrol area and furthermore it was a matter of interfering in another collection. In those days collection boundaries were very jealously guarded – a strange state of affairs when territorial rights seemed to be of greater importance than the successful prevention of smuggling.

In 1823 a Dutch galliott (the usual name for a small Dutch trading vessel that was shaped like a barge), the *Young Fanny*, which was bound from Amsterdam to Bristol with a cargo of bark for tanning leather, anchored in Woodspring Bay. Its very presence in   95 the Bay aroused a certain suspicion as it was not recognised as a place of shelter, most vessels on this stretch of coast used Uphill. A gale sprang up and the vessel was driven onto the headland and was wrecked. The Receiver of Wrecks at Uphill (none other than the Customs tide-waiter) commented on the rather suspicious nature of the circumstances. However, he had to admit that no illegal goods were recovered from the wreck – they may, of course, have already been landed. Eventually most of the ship's equipment and cargo was auctioned at Worle Inn.

The village of Worle is situated on the north-east corner of Worleberry Hill and now is a heavily developed residential suburb of Weston-super-Mare. In the late 18th century it was larger than Weston and had a long tradition of fishing. The village was conveniently placed on the road to Bristol and was quite possibly the centre of smuggling activities in the area. Legend has it that the tower of the village church was used to hide smuggled goods; though most churches near to the coast seemed to acquire such reputations. Kewstoke church, which is even closer to Woodspring and Sand Bays, was also said to have been used by the smugglers. In cases like this it is almost impossible to separate romantic fiction from fact.

And much the same may be said for Weston-super-Mare itself. Local writers have suggested that smuggling flourished along 'its quiet shores' and their comments are larded with the usual romantic overtones of flashing lights, goods hidden in sand-dunes, desperate chases with the Excise et al. There is very little hard evidence to support this view but that does not necessarily mean that there was no smuggling along the shores, by experience one realises that there is no smoke without a fire!

In theory at least, Weston-super-Mare was an ideal spot for the illegal trade. The sands of Weston Bay and its near neighbour, Sand Bay, now much beloved by summer visitors, would have been heaven-sent for the smugglers; indeed they are the only extensive sandy beaches along the whole of the Avon coastline. The village of Weston-super-Mare, and it was nothing more than this until the 1820s when it began to develop as a seaside resort, had long been occupied with fishing. Birnbeck Island to the north of the resort, now joined to the mainland by its Victorian pier, was an ancient fishery. It is a fair assumption to make that most fishermen interested themselves in the smuggling trade to a greater or lesser degree, if only as a means to augment their rather precarious living.

A somewhat added bonus, as far as the illegal trade was concerned, was the nearness of the two islands – Flat and Steep Holm – both well-known as smuggling haunts throughout the 18th century.

Steep Holm, about three miles off-shore, has a very accessible beach to land goods and once boasted an inn. There is no doubt that it was used as a smuggling depot and as it is just about three hours' row from Weston, some of the goods must have found their way to Weston-super-Mare. Flat Holm, some two miles north of Steep Holm, had an even greater reputation for smuggling, as we will see later. It has a cave, which is still called 'Smugglers' Hole'. In 1810 a vessel named the *Rebecca* was wrecked near Steep Holm and much of its cargo was finally washed up onto the beach at Weston. It was reported that 'the farmers carried away milk pails of spirit', which at least shows a willingness of the locals to partake in an illegal bounty!

The only port of any consequence along this coast is Uphill, which is situated at the mouth of the river Axe and nestling under the shelter of Brean Down. Uphill had long been used as a port of haven and had, at one time, an appreciable trade across the Channel with the Welsh ports. It is quite possible that the Romans first established the port to transport the lead mined at Charterhouse in the nearby Mendips. For many, many years a Customs officer was stationed at this creek, a sure sign not only of a steady legal trade but also the recognition of an illegal trade in the area that warranted a Customs 'presence'. The officer came under the control of the Collector at Bristol and was at the furthermost point of his 'empire', and like most wide-spread empires their weakest links were at the outposts, perhaps another reason to support the view that Weston was well used by the smugglers – the coast was not very adequately guarded.

In 1780 a French vessel appeared in Weston Bay at high tide and just proceeded to off-load kegs of brandy. The tide went out and visitors to the resort will know only too well how far the tide recedes at Weston! By morning the sea was almost half a mile away and the hapless vessel was stranded high and dry on the mud. The officer at Uphill sent an urgent message to Bristol for assistance to capture the smuggling vessel, but before help could arrive the vessel had made its escape on the next tide. A good example of how local knowledge of the coast and its tides was essential to a successful smuggling run.

Only a few isolated reports of smuggling have survived. In 1801 a fishing smack from Weston was seized by the Excise for having six ankers of brandy and a quantity of tobacco hidden on board under the catch of fish. The Excise cutter *Lively* had discovered the fishing vessel just off Flat Holm and though a search was made of the island by the Excisemen no other goods were found. What finally happened to the fishing vessel is not recorded. The Excise cutters did not have to worry about collection boundaries, their terms of reference were far wider, for instance the *Lively* could cruise from Falmouth to Bristol, including the Welsh coast. By and large Excise cutters were more successful than their Customs counterparts. The *Lively* had previously served in the English Channel from Dover and had experienced several battles with smuggling vessels so its new area of patrol would seem quite tame in comparison.

Few individual names of smugglers have survived in this area, but a certain John Pitts, who was a regular market carrier to Bristol, was convicted of smuggling a quantity of wine and some tobacco. Norris, the tide-waiter at Uphill, considered Pitts an habitual offender though there is no evidence that he was caught again. Pitts came from Wick St Lawrence, a small village and tiny port, which was close to Woodspring Bay. General carriers like Pitts were always suspect and they had to run the risk of being stopped and their cart searched by Excise officers well inland. For instance, in 1810 the Excise officer at Axbridge seized smuggled linens and silks from a hawker and pedlar named Thomas Wright some twelve miles inland, which gives some idea of the method of distribution of smuggled goods. The risks tradesmen like Wright ran must not be minimised; they were required to be licensed by the Excise and if caught with smuggled goods they frequently had their licence removed, and thus their sole means of livelihood, and ended up in a debtor's prison.

As to the unconfirmed rumours that exist about Weston-super-Mare's smuggling past. Kegs of brandy were said to be frequently hidden in the sand-dunes or 'tots' (as they were known locally) near to where the Winter Gardens are now situated. Brean Down was reputed to be a safe landing place and the smuggled goods transported to Weston by means of a coffin. This is a story that can be found on many other parts of the coast. Certainly in 1818 six casks of brandy were washed up on Brean Down and they were thought to have come from 'a large cutter which had anchored near Steep Holm'. There was an inn near the foreshore which was known as the Half Way House (it later became a hotel and then a sanatorium) which had a reputation as a depot for smuggled goods. I consider that on balance Weston-super-Mare deserves its smuggling reputation and that smuggling was carried on most successfully, judging by the absence of many seizures.

The Somerset coast proper now commences at Brean Down – the mile long promontory which resembles an accusatory finger pointed at Steep Holm. It is also interesting to note that many writers have considered that at this point 'The West Country' starts. The long Berrow Strand of sandhills and dunes stretches away due south for almost six miles. Though today it is covered with chalets and caravans, in previous times it was a wild deserted spot and in theory, at least, a perfect place for landing smuggled goods. However, the area has no smuggling associations, mainly because the coast is more than adequately 'guarded' by the notorious Gore Sands, which have been the final resting place of many a fine sailing ship and poor mariner. Burnham's rather quaint lighthouse on legs is an ever-present reminder of the dangers of these waters.

The turgid and muddy estuaries of the rivers Parrett and Bene with their seemingly aimless meanderings are in themselves a sufficient deterrent to any organised smuggling. These muddy estuaries but herald the famous Somerset Levels, where for centuries a continual battle has been waged to keep the Channel waters at bay. The majority of the hinterland is below the high tide level. The mud found in these estuaries is of a particularly thick and viscous nature that creates problems merely to walk upon let alone to permit the landing of any goods.

So it is not until one reaches what can be called the Quantock shore that smuggling again appeared to prosper. The old and long established ports of Watchet, Minehead and to a lesser extent Porlock provided a regular flow of vessels to and from Ireland and more especially cross-Channel, which encouraged the illegal trade. Watchet and Minehead are directly opposite the South Glamorgan coast and the then smuggling havens of Aberthaw, Sully and Barry Islands. From Minehead the coastline becomes far more dramatic, as indeed do the smuggling legends and stories. The name of the town is said to be derived from the Welsh word for a mountain, 'mynydd', and certainly the town and its port nestles comfortably under the shelter of a formidable hill which merely heralds the awesome cliffs that dominate the coastal scenery right along to Baggy Point, the southern extremity of Morte Bay.

Also from Minehead starts the Somerset and North Devon coastal path that can be walked the 70 or so miles to Hartland Point, where the Bristol Channel meets the full fury of the Atlantic Ocean. Along this quite splendid route there are ample reminders of the smuggling past: 'smugglers caves', 'brandy paths', 'smugglers look-outs', all abound and there is even a 'smugglers leap', all of which suggest that a most active illegal trade was conducted along the coast throughout the 18th and early 19th centuries.

By comparison the Quantock coast is almost gentle and will be long remembered for its association with Wordsworth and Coleridge. One village that attracted them both was Kilve. It is not quite on the coast but it has, nevertheless, a darker side to its character. It was long noted as a well-known smuggling place. The shore at Kilve is a rather small rocky place surrounded by long, broken cliffs and its sheer beauty inspired the poets – 'On Kilve's smooth shore by the green sea'. Almost due north from Kilve lies Barry Island, which no doubt accounted in some measure for Kilve's smuggling reputation.

Despite its fame, or notoriety, there are only two recorded seizures of smuggled goods near the village. In 1773 an Excise ride-officer from Bridgwater found four bales of tobacco and two kegs of spirits, 'hidden in a hedgerow near Kilve'. 'Ride' was an Excise term used to describe an Excise area that could only be controlled on horse-back as compared to the 'foot-walk' areas in and about towns. The ride-officer must not be confused with the Customs riding officers. Eight years later John Merry, a Customs riding officer from Watchet (though he appeared to operate from his home at East Quantox-head), interrupted a landing of goods at Kilve. The offending vessel was thought to have come from Aberthaw, just across the Channel, with a cargo of lime and coal. It made its escape, as did most of the landers with the majority of the smuggled goods. Merry was left with just two packages of tea and one cask of brandy 'badly damaged by the sea', which usually meant that the spirit had been contaminated by salt-water. Merry spent a rather abortive couple of days searching the surrounding area for some trace of the other goods but with no success. One wonders whether he examined the ruins of the 12th century chantry at Kilve, which had a reputation that it was once 'the home of smugglers'. Merry's Collector at Bridgwater commented in his report to London that an Excise boat should be used to patrol the coast, as the 'country people are most impudent in the way they abuse the King's revenue . . . . and scarce does a week past [sic] but my officers do hear of goods being landed on the shore. It is firmly believed that they come from across the Sea carryed by the colliers that trade regularly to the kilns . . .' The Excise collector could not resist making a sly dig at the Customs, he averred 'the coast hereabouts is barely patrolled by the officers of the Customs for what reason I know not'!

All this happened before the two poets lived in the area. However, one does wonder whether they witnessed any smuggling activities during their frequent excursions along the coast, especially as during the 1790s smuggling can be said to have been at its height. It is interesting to note also that the two poets created so much interest and suspicion that it was felt that they were French spies. Indeed the Home Office treated the matter so seriously that they sent one of their men – a Mr G. Walsh – to investigate them. Walsh followed the poets on their rambles and hid behind sand-dunes in an attempt to listen to their conversations. No doubt the smuggling fraternity would have thought Walsh to be a Customs man if they had found him acting in such a suspicious manner. Considering that the poets were completely exonerated, one is tempted to comment that Walsh would have been more gainfully employed spying on the smugglers – alas there was no co-operation between Government departments.

There is only one other reference to smuggling in the area and this was in 1851 when nine casks of spirits were seized by the Coast-guard. It would appear that they had drifted in on the tide close to Quantoxhead. Several days later another cask was found concealed in a ditch and this was found to be almost empty. A local farm labourer was found dead quite close by, but whether there was any connection is open to conjecture. It is worth noting that most of the smuggled spirits were very strong and fiery, most were well over 100% proof spirit (at present the legal limit for the sale of spirits is 70%). The idea, of course, was to add water to the spirits, not only to increase the quantity but also to make them more drinkable. It was even reputed that special caramel colouring was also smuggled from France to be added to the diluted smuggled brandy so that it would retain its 'colour'.

Watchet is the only small Bristol Channel port to have managed a resurgence as a commercial port; it now has a most respectable foreign trade with Portugal and the Mediterranean. However, when Defoe visited the port in the 1720s he found it 'a miserable stinking place, which like a withered beauty, has only now to boast that it was once handsome'. The main trade during the 18th century was the export of kelp (a seaweed used in glass making) and gypsum – a kind of alabaster used for making plaster of Paris – and, of course, the inevitable import of lime and culm (small coal). There were literally dozens of lime kilns along the Somerset and Devon coasts, most of them actually sited on the beaches or very adjacent to the shore. Numerous coastal smacks brought the limestone and culm from Aberthaw and other Welsh ports and ponies with panniers were used to transport the material away – some of the lime was used on the land to improve its condition. Because of the unusual Channel tides and the fact that the vessels were unloading their cargoes onto open beaches it was a most hazardous operation needing a very speedy discharge. Therefore it was a perfect scenario for smuggling. The vessels came from a notorious smuggling area, transport was ready on hand to move the smuggled goods and because the beaches were so remote there was very little danger of discovery.

101

As early as 1682 Watchet had gained an unenviable reputation for its illegal trade. The Customs Board sent their Surveyor-General, William Culliford, to inspect the port and its near neighbour Minehead. Culliford, without doubt, was the most able Customs official of his time. He later set up the machinery to collate official statistics of imports and exports (the earliest Balance of Payments) and for all his good work he was appointed Commissioner. Culliford found the port to be in a deplorable state; the Collector – William Dashwood – spent most of his time drinking 'sack' with the ships' captains whilst cargoes of brandies and wines were being landed in the harbour without payment of duties. He also found that some vessels imported only illegal cargoes, with Dashwood, of course, taking his share. It would appear that there was virtually no Customs control in operation. Dashwood was suspended from duty and replaced by his deputy, who had originally informed on him. Dashwood's brother, Samuel, was an Excise collector in Norfolk, he too was suspended for 'misuse of His Majesty's Excise' – bad blood somewhere?

During 1735 the landing-waiter at the port seized spirits and tobacco from the *Good Intent*, which had arrived from Aberthaw. The goods had been landed 'by the harbour wall at the dead of night', which shows a certain dedication to duty on behalf of the Customs man! The master of the vessel, Thomas Niall, was fined a mere £5, he was very fortunate not to have his vessel seized. Some ten years later 'a small collier from Neath' put into the harbour under stress of weather. Six casks of brandy and some packages of tobacco were found on board. The master, William Smith, stoutly maintained that he had found the goods 'floating off Flat Holm' and that he was going to hand them over to the Customs! The goods were seized but there is no report to show whether the master's story was believed or not, certainly the vessel was not confiscated so it does seem most likely that he got away with his very tall story.

The 1780s seemed to be quite productive for the Customs, there were quite a few seizures made in and around Watchet. More often than not they were very small quantities – one or two kegs of brandy and the odd package of tea or tobacco. Most of the goods were either picked up along the shore or else found hidden in the hedgerows. However, in 1784, the Excise officers uncovered a large cache of brandy and wines in 'an outbuilding not a mile from Dunster'. The goods were taken to Taunton for public auction and they were sold for £173. This seizure resulted in a bitter dispute between the Excise and the Customs. Thomas Broad, a Customs riding officer at Blue Anchor (a small port close to Watchet) claimed a share of the seizure reward on the grounds that he had told the local Excise officer where the goods were hidden – he did not explain why he did not seize them himself. The Excise countered with the allegation that Broad was in collusion with the smugglers and, because he was not receiving his fair share, he had decided to inform on them. Unfortunately the final outcome of this dispute is not known as the reply from the Excise Board in London is missing. Such disputes were quite frequent and there are similar examples on other parts of the coast.

Minehead, as a port, prospered as Watchet and Porlock declined. For most of the period under review there was a Customs Collector at the port to control the not inconsiderable trade with Ireland and other foreign parts. In 1670 the Custom House was robbed, though there are dark hints that it had been 'an inside job' as one of the officers was later suspended for 'deficiencies of monies belonging to His Majesty'. Twelve years later Culliford inspected the port and although he found it in a better state than Watchet, he did report that 'free-trading' was in the ascendancy and considered that it was actively encouraged by the local merchants and landowners. As a local historian has written '. . . The Country gentry had no objection to the flavour of the brandy that had paid no duty and they slept no less comfortably because the sheets of Irish linen had escaped the King's officers.'

There are few recorded seizures of smuggled goods in the port, perhaps because it was always well-controlled with a staff of six officers of various grades, which seems quite a number for what was a relatively small port. Also what was the point of taking an unnecessary risk of capture when there were plenty of suitable landing places on the coasts either side of the port. In 1738 Thomas Beynon (he sounds like an immigrant from across the Channel!), a boatman at the port, discovered 'a gig at the beach', which was loaded with six casks of brandy. Beynon felt that the goods had come from the *Emma* of Porlock, a vessel which traded with Ireland and Bristol. The vessel was searched by the Customs and six bales of Irish linen was found 'under the sheets'. The vessel was placed under detention until a decision was made by London. It was almost two months later when the reply arrived at the port. The master was fined £10, which he gladly paid and his vessel was released. In those days the penalties for smuggling were relatively light compared with those imposed just a decade or so later.

Just six years later the Collector received a letter from London informing him that smuggling was on the increase – in fact all the Customs collectors in the Bristol Channel were similarly informed. 103

However, the Minehead collector decided to issue an order to all his staff, mainly, I feel, for the benefit of those riding officers who covered the coasts either side of the port:

> '. . . there have been several instances of runs along our coasts and you are commanded to show your utmost diligence in your duties to patrol regularly and to watch the known places of landing by day and by night. You are ordered to give especial attention to those vessels that trade with the Welch [sic] coast. All informations that you learn by way of business is to be conveyed to your superior officers at your earliest and all possible speede. Further you are to patrol at irregular times of the day and night without consideration to your private business and strictly record such visits in your journals, which will be inspected by your superior officer.'

Perhaps as a result of this sharp reminder of their duties, there was a rash of seizures. A fishing vessel from Ilfracombe was seized near Greenleigh Point, some two miles west of the port, with a quantity of 'forraign salt' on board as well as two ankers of brandy and Irish goods. It is interesting to note that earlier Ordnance Survey maps indicate a smugglers' cave near to this spot. Much closer to the port, ten kegs of spirit and two boxes of tea were found hidden near Warren Point, which is quite close to the present golf club and not a stone's throw from Butlin's holiday complex. The Customs were convinced that these goods had come from a Bristol-bound vessel, which had made a brief call at the port on route up the Channel. The suspect vessel was the *Western Star* and so confident were the local staff that the master was responsible that a message was sent to the Bristol collector to pay particular attention to the vessel whilst it was unloading at Bristol. There is no evidence that any further seizures were made from this vessel, if indeed the Bristol officers took any notice of the warning. However, such action showed a changed Customs mentality; if only this spirit of co-operation had taken place earlier perhaps the Customs would have been a little more successful in their operations instead of jealously guarding their boundaries.

During the next 20 years there were several instances of small packages of goods (mainly tobacco) being washed up on the shore, none of the quantities were of much significance and indeed nowhere along both the Somerset and Avon coasts do any large smuggling figures emerge, which would suggest that the majority of smuggling was undertaken by small and regular trading vessels from across the Channel and also from fishing vessels, which were always suspect.

However, in 1771, a large smuggling run was *thought* to have taken place at Dunster beach. Quite obviously the Customs in Minehead had received prior information about the run because officers from

Minehead searched the country around Dunster for two days without finding any trace of the goods. The collector at Minehead was of the opinion that the goods had been landed from a foreign vessel outward bound from Bristol and 'had been guided to the place by the pilot, who are all known smugglers'. He further made the point that 'without the provision of a proper boat to guard the coast, we are unable to counter the pernicious trade'.

One can understand the Collector's problems; the coast to Hurleston Point, some six miles to the west of Minehead, is quite inaccessible today, let alone 200 years ago. A writer in 1791 described it as '. . . a grand scene of craggy and romantic rocks . . . the cliffs on the East side of this point [Hurleston] hang over the beach with aweful sublimity and grandeur . . .' Below the Point is Bossington, which has a rocky beach and the ruins of two lime kilns. Here came the little trading smacks from Wales with lime and culm. They would beach at high tide and then have a mere twelve hours to discharge their cargo before the next tide. Only two seizures were recorded at this spot, both on vessels from 'the opposite shore'. The *Mari* from Aberthaw was only 15 tons and its master and owner Thomas James was fined £40 for landing a mere anker of brandy and four pounds of tea. The name of the other vessel has not survived, merely 'a smack from Swansey', which had landed three bales of tobacco and some linen goods. As the nearest Customs official was stationed at Porlock Weir, some three miles away along the stretch of Porlock beach, Bossington would appear to be a safe landing place and no doubt many, many consignments were landed here and spirited away in the panniers of the ponies long before any official could be at the spot.

The port of Porlock Weir is now used almost exclusively by yachtsmen and although Defoe dismissed it as '. . . a small harbour but of no importance, nor has it any thing of trade so I need but name it', nevertheless there was enough legal trade to warrant the presence of a tide-waiter. However, the port was famous for its herring fishery and its shipbuilding. There are ample references to vessels 'of Porlock' using the various Channel ports and a fair percentage of them appeared to be involved in the illegal trade.

For instance in 1765 the *Holly* of Porlock was seized at Ilfracombe for carrying 'six tubs of spirits' hidden under a cargo of fish. At Aberthaw, in 1772, Edward Micheal, the master of the *Two Sisters*, was caught landing packages of tobacco and jars of rum. Indeed he attempted to bribe the Customs officer with a jar of rum! And at Newport in 1790 the *Adventure*, a smack from Porlock, was seized for landing six ankers of brandy and ten packages of tobacco at the entrance to the river Ebbw. It is interesting to note that the *Adventure* had a specially constructed compartment in the bulkhead to hide the goods. As this vessel appeared to be a regular Channel trader, the master and owner, John Thetone, must have carried on a most profitable trade until his ruse was finally discovered by an alert Customs boatman. The two *Ship* inns, one at the Weir and the other in the village of Porlock, no doubt played their part in the old smuggling days but no firm evidence has survived.

The coast from Watchet to Porlock has gained a strong reputation for smuggling, which seems to be hardly supported by the existing

106   An 18th century engraving showing the violence and brutality of smuggling.

evidence. Nevertheless it cannot be dismissed purely on this score. It was a wild and largely uninhabited shore virtually ignored by the Revenue, but it received enough regular traders from across the Channel to fuel a clandestine trade. However, the terrain of the coast dictated the type of illegal trade – no large landing of goods like the south coast – but small and regular shipments brought ashore by the little smacks. Such small-time smuggling was never likely to be accorded much Revenue interest – hence the paucity of Customs seizures. But without doubt the illegal trade flourished along this coast. The perils in navigating the dangerous waters and making a landfall in the small havens were formidable and quite daunting and so one must conclude that the intrepid masters and mariners who used this coast richly deserved such hard-won rewards from a little bit of smuggling on the side!

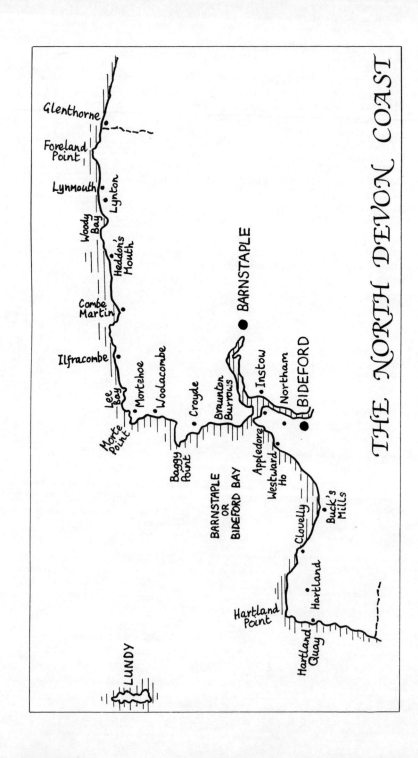

THE NORTH DEVON COAST

Glenthorne
Foreland Point
Lynmouth
Lynton
Woody Bay
Heddon's Mouth
Combe Martin
Ilfracombe
Lee Bay
Morte Point
Mortehoe
Woolacombe
Croyde
Baggy Point
Braunton Burrows
BARNSTAPLE
Instow
Northam
BIDEFORD
BARNSTAPLE OR BIDEFORD BAY
Appledore
Westward Ho
Clovelly
Buck's Mills
Hartland
Hartland Point
Hartland Quay
LUNDY

5

The North Devon Coast

The stretch of coast from Porlock Weir to Ilfracombe is rightly famed for its rich scenic beauty, which can hardly be surpassed in the whole of the West Country. Lynton, Lynmouth, Combe Martin, Heddon's Mouth, Hunters Inn and the Valley of the Rocks have their own devotees and all are places that have attracted tourists and walkers alike for nigh on 200 years. Countless writers have eulogised the splendid beauty of the area – the quite magnificent but awesome towering cliffs above the small rocky inlets, where little sailing ships entered at their peril to discharge their legal cargoes of lime and culm and their illegal cargoes of tobacco and spirits. One Victorian writer was moved to comment, 'To describe the beauty of the cliffs and sea would exhaust our stock of epithets'! This spectacular coastline needs no enhancement but for an added bonus it is backed by Exmoor, that wild and rather secretive land, which imbues the whole area with a special mood and spirit. It lends itself to numerous legends, many of which relate to smuggling.

Amongst the earliest travellers to discover the beauty of this coast were Coleridge, Wordsworth, Southey and Shelley and their associations with the area ensured its popularity. It is from young William Hazlitt, who walked the coast with Coleridge in 1798, that we obtain the first eye-witness impression of the coast at the height of its smuggling days.

'We walked for miles and miles on dark brown heaths overlooking the Channel with the Welsh hills beyond, and at times descended into little sheltered valleys close by the seaside with a smuggler's face scowling at us, and then had to ascend conical hills with a path winding up through a coppice to a barren top, like a monk's shaven crown . . .'

Unlike travellers' tales of smuggling on other coasts, there are no reports of bands of smugglers swaggering along in contempt of authority but rather the odd smuggler, curious and suspicious of all who trespassed along their secret ways. Indeed Hazlitt's description encapsulates the North Devon smugglers – they operated by stealth and subterfuge and not by open defiance like some of their colleagues to the south of the County.

The poets, and indeed any other travellers, were quite fortunate not to have encountered any Customs officials on their walks along the coast, because since 1736 there had been a Smuggling Act in force whereby 'any person or persons found lurking, waiting or loitering within five miles of the sea coast . . . who shall not give a satisfactory account of themselves and their callings and employments shall be committed to the house of correction, there to be whipt and kept to hard labour.' An explanation that they were 'poets' would not have been readily accepted! However, it would have been most unlikely for them to encounter any Revenue official along the coast from Porlock to Lynton (their ultimate destination) as it was, for long periods at least, almost totally devoid of any Revenue protection. Furthermore there is no evidence that 'any person or persons' were ever convicted under this Act; it was really unworkable. The Act was analogous to the more famous 'Hovering Acts' at sea, which empowered the Revenue to seize any vessel of 50 tons or under found 'hovering' within two leagues (about six miles) of the coast. These Acts formed the backbone of smuggling legislation and were sedulously enforced.

The road to Lynton makes a steep ascent out of Porlock, which has in modern times been more than a match for many an aged motor car, and just a mile or so away, near the coast, is a village with a long smuggling tradition – Culbone. The village church is thought to be the smallest parish church in England and by sheer coincidence it is the exact same length as the famous Bristol Channel pilot cutters – 36 feet! Like most churches that are in sight of the sea, it was reputed to have been used to store smuggled goods and I have no doubt that there is more than a grain of truth in the story. The sheltered beach, which is backed by extensive woodlands, provided a good landing place and furthermore a steady trade had been established with several Welsh ports, thus ensuring a regular supply of uncustomed goods.

In 1756 the Naval sloop *Defiance* was making its way to Ilfracombe to take on fresh supplies when an 'Irish wherry' was sighted 'acting rather suspiciously' just to the west of Gore Point (Culbone). An 'unshotted' shot (that is, powder only) was fired across the vessel's bows as a warning for it to heave to ready for inspection – such warning shots were mandatory under the various Smuggling Acts. The wherry did not waste any time, it made all possible sail and hared away. The *Defiance* gave chase but, according to the Commander's report, the smuggling vessel was lost somewhere west of

Lundy. However, not easily baulked, the Commander brought his vessel back to Culbone and put two parties of seamen ashore to search for the landed goods. They found only two badly damaged ankers of brandy and a small quantity of 'sea damaged' tea. The Collector at Ilfracombe who reported the incident to London, commented that 'this particular coast thereabouts is heavily into the trade and is distant from this place [Ilfracombe] as to make its proper protection impossible'. He further pointed out that the officer at Porlock Weir was not 'urgent in his ways'. Porlock Weir was, of course, in the Bristol collection and normally Customs officers were not encouraged to cross boundaries.

The whole coast is heavily wooded even now and in those days it would have been even more so, thus affording excellent protection to any smuggler. This was especially so along to what is now known as Glenthorne, which is on the county boundary between Somerset and Devon. In 1820 it was described as 'a wild place . . . the rendezvous of smugglers', and what is more its hinterland is now famous as 'Doone Country'. Blackmore used many of the stories and legends prevalent in the area in his unforgettable story *Lorna Doone*. The only positive evidence of smuggling at Glenthorne happened in 1813 when the preventive boat, which was based at Countisbury cove barely a mile or so west of the village, picked up six ankers of brandy that had been sunk just off the coast. The crew landed on the shore and made a thorough search of the shoreline but did not find a trace of any other goods. There is a path near Countisbury which is still known today as 'Brandy Path'.

Slightly further inland, at Brendon in 1818 a packman named John Whittle was fined £10 for smuggling and also sentenced to six months hard labour for assaulting an Excise officer. It is not recorded just what goods he was smuggling. And even further afield an Excise officer stopped a carrier, Joseph Black, on the road out of South Molton during March 1824. The cart was well laden with 'market goods', but underneath were hidden two ankers of brandy and 'several empty bottles'. It would appear that Black was in the habit of selling the brandy by the bottle, which would have brought him in a vastly increased profit. According to the Excise officer, 'there was no permit'. Duty-paid spirits required a permit signed by an Excise officer before being conveyed from place to place however short the distance. Permits were introduced in an attempt to control the movement of smuggled spirits but it was a woefully inept system. The two ankers and the cart were seized and Black was fined £50 for smuggling – a very considerable sum in those days. Indeed invariably most convicted smugglers could not pay the penalty and were imprisoned for debt to the Crown. Many spent years in prison and some did not survive the ordeal. In the case of Black it does seem a very harsh penalty for what was in fact petty smuggling – a savage fine and the loss of his livelihood. However, this seizure clearly shows the long tentacles of smuggled goods throughout the country.

Some of the most intrepid travellers and walkers of the 19th century and earlier were clergymen. The Rev. Richard Warner, who travelled the West Country during 1790/1800s, has left some vivid descriptions of the country at that time, but none, alas, of the smuggling trade. However, over a century later, another clergyman W. H. Thorton recorded a meeting with an octogenarian smuggler, who was probably involved in the illegal trade during the early decades of the century:

'. . . I sat by the deathbed of a very old smuggler, who told me how he used to have a donkey with a triangle on its back so rigged up to show three lanthorns and how chilled he would become as he lay out on a winter's night, watching on the Foreland [Foreland Point between Countisbury Cove and Lynton, some 725 feet high and thus giving wonderful views over the coast and across the Channel – a perfect look-out spot] or along Brandy path, as we called it, for the three triangular lights of the schooner, which he knew was coming in to land her cargo where Glenthorne now stands and where there was a smuggler's cave. "Lord bless yer, sir," and the dying man of nearly ninety years chuckled, "we never used no water, we just put the brandy into a kettle and heated it and drinked it out of half-pint stoups [flagons or beakers] us did and it never did us no harm whatsoever, it was of that quality, it were . . ."'

A rather delightful story of 'the good old days of smuggling', but I feel that distant memory has lent some enchantment to the view. There was no doubt that smuggling was a hard, arduous and dangerous business and by the early 1820s the risk of capture was quite high and not many individuals made much money out of the trade. Furthermore by this time most of the smuggled goods were being sunk just off the shore and left until it was felt safe to recover them. 'Sowing the crop' was the term used for sinking the ankers and 'harvesting' for their recovery. Fairly often the casks suffered from seepage of salt-water, indeed it is thought that the origin of 'shrub' – a cordial of fruit juice and spirits – derived from the use of herbs and spices added to tainted spirits to make them more drinkable.

Lynton and Lynmouth, to the west of Foreland Point, are rightly praised for their scenic beauty and they have been likened to an English Switzerland. For most of the 18th century they were very isolated communities, their life-line was the herring fishery and the sea. Much of the trade of Lynmouth was to supply goods by sea rather than by the long and expensive overland route. For most of the time there was no permanent Customs officer at the port, officers would come over from Ilfracombe to clear any cargoes, except in the case of coal and culm. The port had its own part-time 'coal meter' – whose sole duty was to weigh coal to ascertain the quantity for payment of the coastwise duties. Because such officials did not hold a commission they could not seize any goods and therefore were of no preventive use or value. The last incumbent in the post at Lynton was a local publican, perhaps at *The Rising Sun*, which had a reputation as a smuggling pub!

The Collector at Ilfracombe frequently reported that Lynmouth was thought to be deeply involved in the smuggling trade but it was not until 1805 that a riding officer was based there. Nevertheless there were precious few recorded seizures of note, the occasional cask of brandy 'found on the shore' or 'hidden in a hedgerow', but sufficient pointers to suggest that some smuggling was taking place.

It was in 1809 that the largest smuggling run was discovered. The excise cutter *Resolution*, which was based in Milford Haven, was patrolling the Devon coast when 'a large smuggling lugger' was sighted. William Lilburn, the Commander of the *Resolution*, was a very experienced Revenue officer who had served at Dover where smuggling was of the real 'blood and thunder' variety, and he decided to give chase to the lugger. In a sea-mist the lugger, the *Mary Ann* of Fowey, managed to evade the Excise cutter for sufficient time to land some 600 ankers of brandy. When Lilburn located the lugger she was aground near Lynmouth. Lilburn was torn between securing the vessel and landing a party of men to seize the goods. He decided the vessel was a greater prize and brought it into Ilfracombe before returning to Lynmouth to search for the goods. However, almost 48 hours had elapsed and not surprisingly not one cask was recovered. In his report to the Excise Board in London Lilburn had some harsh words to say about the riding officer at Lynmouth; he inferred that the officer was in collusion with the smugglers. In mitigation of the poor officer one must state that to live and work in such an isolated community as the sole upholder of law and order was not a particularly enviable position to be in – discretion was often the better part of valour.

The last riding officer stationed at Lynmouth in 1832 was Michael Sullivan and he seized three horses carrying 64 kegs of spirits along Countisbury Common. The two men leading the horses were both farm labourers, they did not know how the goods had been landed or

113

indeed who owned the horses. They said that they had been employed merely to pick up the consignment at a certain spot and leave it 'at the cross-roads on the road to Brendon'! The only information that was subsequently discovered was that the goods had been landed at Countisbury Cove and that 'a gentleman's yacht' had been used. The two farm labourers were convicted of smuggling and their fines were paid, so perhaps 'the gentleman' had come to their aid?

It is less than 20 miles from Lynton to Ilfracombe but because of its terrain it seems much longer. It is perhaps the most majestic and dramatic scenery along the whole of the Bristol Channel. It does also have its full measure of smuggling lore but again, like so many other parts of the coast, there is very little hard evidence to back up the reputation. At Lee Valley there is a delightful little bay with the inevitable ruined lime kiln; these kilns are so much a feature of this coast – in fact at one time there were no less than 18 kilns near Combe Martin. Lee Valley is overlooked by a headland bearing the name Duty Point and it was here that one of the first Coastguard stations was established in 1822 – reason enough to believe the smuggling tales.

The only recorded Revenue success was the seizure of a quantity of tobacco and spirits from a small smack, the *Sunrise* from Aberthaw with lime and culm. The owner and master managed to escape from the preventive boat that came from Heddon's Mouth. On the cliff-path out of the Bay there is a spot known as 'Smuggler's leap', where legend has it that a smuggler was being chased by a Revenue officer. They were both on horseback and in the struggle both toppled to their deaths.

Heddon's Mouth is another of the many places that had a fine reputation as a landing place for smuggled goods. The first noted seizure here was in 1786, when an 'Irish wherry' discharged a cargo of spirits and tobacco onto the shore. But before most of the goods could be spirited away a party of Customs men descended onto the beach and managed, despite opposition, to secure 20 ankers of spirit and 13 bales of tobacco. The vessel made its escape as did all of the landing party, for nobody was convicted. This is one of the very rare instances in smuggling on this side of the Channel where there was a direct confrontation between a body of Customs officers and smugglers. Another interesting point was that the vessel was believed to belong to Knight of Lundy. This is the famous smuggler of Barry Island whom we will meet later.

In May 1799 a cutter called the *Hope*, reputedly from Appledore, landed no less than 96 ankers of brandy at Heddon's Mouth and then moved further west to Watermouth, beyond Combe Martin, to land the rest of its cargo – some 80 ankers. However, the master misjudged his bearings and came in rather too close to the shore; the vessel ran onto rocks, sank and all hands were lost. It is strange that this should happen because the small harbour of Watermouth was considered one of the safest along the coast. A tide-waiter was regularly employed at the harbour to collect the duties on coal and culm used in the lime kiln situated near the shore. In 1802 George Fishley, the officer then serving at the little port, found a large puncheon of rum – nearly 100 gallons in all – hidden in an outhouse. How it had been landed (not an easy task) or to whom it belonged was never discovered, though Fishley thought that one of the Channel pilot boats was the culprit – it would seem that the pilots were used as general scapegoats! There are several caves in the area that were thought to have been used by smugglers and the next bay along from Watermouth is called Samson's Bay, which is said to have been named after a local smuggler who used the bay, though nothing can be found out about him.

Trentishoe and its neighbouring hamlet of Martinhoe are situated in a lonely, sheltered valley but close to the sea and one can quite easily understand just how they gained their smuggling reputations. The little church at Martinhoe – only three feet longer than Culbone – was no doubt used to hide smuggled goods. Indeed there is an entry in the parish register against the recorded death of one Dick Jones at the grand age of 103 – 'the last of the smugglers'! One is forced to comment that the long, cold nights on the shore or the hot brandy did not seem to do him much harm!

Ilfracombe is the longest established and, indeed, the most important port along the Exmoor coast. It first came into prominence as a harbour of refuge, as probably the safest spot along the whole of the south side of the Bristol Channel. One 18th century visitor described it as 'a beautiful natural basin sheltered by craggy heights'. The port developed a flourishing trade with Ireland, Bristol, Falmouth (a notorious smuggling port) and the Welsh ports, especially Swansea. This latter trade link quickly developed into a regular ferry service. The port also boasted a fine reputation for shipbuilding which continued up to the middle of the last century, but by this time it was fast developing as a seaside resort of some distinction. George Eliot stayed there for a short period in the summer of 1856 and left many descriptions of the town and surrounding area:

'. . . The view [from the Torrs] is perhaps the finest to be had at Ilfracombe. Bay behind bay, fringed with foam, promontory behind   115 promontory, each with its peculiar shades of purple light – the sweep of the Welsh coast faintly visible in the distance and the endless expanse of sea . . .'

She left the town for Tenby and went by way of the Swansea ferry, the crossing taking one whole day.

Originally, in the 17th century, the port was under the control of the Customs Collector at Exeter but by 1678 it was of sufficient importance to have its own Collector. By 1700 one of the first Customs smacks was stationed at the port, which not only showed its growing importance but also the concern for smuggling in that part of the Channel. With Lundy Island not too far to the west of the port this is not surprising. In 1781 the Collector Peter Fosse reported to London:

'We have received intelligence from undoubted authority that large quantities of tea and brandy are frequently discharged out of Armed Smugglers from France and lodged on the Island of Lundy till opportunities offer of putting the same on board Pilot Boats belonging to the Port.'

The port was not only used by the Bristol Channel pilots, since it was a very convenient base to meet the incoming vessels just west of Lundy, but also the port's mariners acted as unofficial pilots without licences. Both groups brought back smuggled goods to the port, often quite openly and there were many seizures of tea, brandy and sugar – the latter from West Indiamen trading to Bristol.

One local vessel that seemed to be a continual thorn in the side of the Customs was the *Cornwall*, which regularly went out to meet the incoming vessels in the Channel. Frequently it was rummaged by the Customs but, as on each occasion no smuggled goods were found, it would appear that the master was given prior knowledge of these searches. Just once some illegal goods were found on board but, because they were not hidden, the master was fined but the vessel was not forfeited. However, in 1782 four half-ankers of brandy were found on board and a closer search disclosed six bags of tea hidden under the forecastle. This time the vessel was seized and ultimately condemned, suffering the usual fate – it was sawn into three pieces. It had been owned by William Arthur of Pennard in the Gower – one of the most notorious smugglers in the Channel, of whom more later.

The Collector continually complained to the Board in London about the increase of smuggling on the coast. He rightly pointed out that his staff, which only numbered four, could not possibly contain the illegal trade, especially as they were not armed and furthermore the nearest troops were 50 miles distant. However, in 1787 a Revenue cutter was once again stationed at the port. It was called the *Fox* – an ex-smuggling vessel from Plymouth, it was a small vessel less than 50 tons and carried four two-pounder guns. But during the short period it was at the port, less than three years, no seizure of note was made and it was moved to the south coast where smuggling was rampant.

The Excise cutter *Ferret*, which was based at Milford, had far greater success. It had a wide-ranging role and was able to patrol most of the Channel and its approaches. The first seizure near Ilfracombe was the sloop *Success* of Padstow – over 1,000 pounds of manufactured tobacco and nearly 300 pounds of snuff, all neatly packed in waterproof bladders ready for sinking, were seized. And in May 1791 the Cardiff collier *Polly* was caught with 500 pounds of tobacco. Before the summer was out a small smack from Mevagissey in Cornwall was picked up 'hovering' near the coast to the east of Ilfracombe and a quantity of gin and brandy was seized. To round off a most successful season the *Morning Star*, an open pilot gig, was caught with 250 pounds of tobacco and a quantity of cigars, which had been bought from a Spanish vessel outward bound from Bristol. The tobacco and cigars had been exported duty-free from Bristol just a few days earlier and but for the seizure could have been back in circulation on the mainland in less than a week. All the condemned cargoes were brought back to Ilfracombe and sold by public auction.

Quite frequently Naval vessels came into Ilfracombe either because of stress of weather or to replenish their stores. In 1800 the Naval cutter *Dover* seized the *Endeavour* of Bideford with considerable quantities of brandy, gin, rum and salt. The vessel had been found hovering off Brandy Cove – rather appropriately named – just a mile or so to the west of the port. This was one of the rare occasions when a condemned vessel was not destroyed, it was offered up for sale at public auction and ended up as a fishing boat. The reason it was sold was that it was not considered 'fast enough for the smuggling trade'. The logic behind this decision seems rather odd considering it had been caught smuggling in the first place. One wonders whether its new owner used it in the smuggling trade?

During 1800 the Collector made a strong plea for extra staff to help combat the illegal trade. He enumerated the parts of the coast that he considered were particularly vulnerable – Heddon's Mouth, Lynmouth, Countisbury, Samson and Lee Bays. The latter place is about four miles west of Ilfracombe. The approach to the Bay is from high moorland down a delightful and secluded valley, well- 117

A Smuggler and *The Preventive Service*, two prints of the 1830s when the modern Coastguard Service, which brought about the end of smuggling, was formed.

wooded, which opens onto a sandy and rocky shore; almost perfectly designed by nature for smuggling. There is a listed building on the edge of the shore, which is reputed to be a smuggler's cottage and it bears the date '1627'. It was at this Bay that the local smuggling hero operated. Hannibal Richards (they never seemed to have ordinary names!) was well-known to the Collector. His name appears in several reports but like all good smugglers he was never convicted. He is thought to have come from Morwenstow in North

Cornwall and gained his early experience in the smuggling trade with the Coppinger gang. It is impossible to even surmise how active he was but it seems most unlikely that his operations were on the scale of smuggling kings like Gulliver or Henry Carter on the south coast. However, he did live to a ripe old age and died of natural causes.

The Collector's appeal for extra staff did not go unheeded because in 1801 James Harper was appointed riding officer at Lee. His patrol was the ten miles to Bideford Bar, but one condition of his appointment was that he was compelled to live 'in or near Lee Bay'.

Besides the continual problems with the pilot boats operating

119

round and from Lundy and the incursions on the coasts, the collector and his small staff had to contend with a variety of vessels that used the port of Ilfracombe for urgent repairs or as a haven during bad weather. More often than not smuggled goods were landed from these vessels whilst they were in the harbour. Reports of brandy, rice, rum, calico, tea and wines coming ashore at the dead of night virtually in sight of the Custom House were fairly frequent, but usually the Customs only heard about the landings from informers after the event, when the officers could do little or nothing about them.

However, in 1817, the officers were more fortunate. They patiently watched whilst 300 gallons of rum, 1,000 pounds of tobacco and over 500 gallons of wines were being transported out of a Bristol vessel, the *Margaret Jane*, all in the early hours of the morning. The vessel had been en route to Bristol from the West Indies and had been compelled to put in to Ilfracombe for urgent repairs, as it had been badly damaged in an Atlantic storm. The owners and master of the *Margaret Jane* received heavy penalties but the seamen caught landing the goods were given the option of either a prison sentence or impressment into the Navy; it is not recorded what choice they made! Only two years earlier the collector had been unwise enough to commit to paper his views on the state of smuggling in his domain: 'the illegal trade has greatly lessened on this coast and it is my belief that it will not ever revive'! Rather wishful thinking and really anticipating a situation that was not to prevail for another 30 years or so.

The Collector's jurisdiction ended at Morte Point and from here the Collector at Barnstaple assumed responsibility. Morte Point, a rugged headland, had gained notoriety because of the dangerous sunken reef of rocks to the westward of the Point. These were marked on maps and charts as 'Morte Stone', but they were more commonly known as 'The Stones of Death' on account of the number of vessels that had come to grief at the spot; not for nothing was the area dubbed 'The Cruel Coast'. Even the Barnstaple Bar – a large sandbank that guards the entrance to the estuaries of the rivers Taw and Torridge – had long taken a heavy toll of shipping and it was the considered opinion of the Admiralty that the loss of lives and vessels in the Bay exceeded that of any portion of the coast of the United Kingdom.

Charles Kingsley, writing in 1849, had something to say about the wrecking habits of the local people; 'Wild folk are these here, gatherers of shellfish and laver [a strange similarity to the Gower coast just across the Channel] and merciless to wrecked vessels, which they consider as their own by some immemorial usage or rather divine right.' However, life was very hard, eking out a living from the land and goods washed up on the shore would seem like providence from God. As a local poet wrote of a later wreck, 'The *John and Lilley* came Ashore To feed the hungry and clothe the poor.' Nevertheless where there were wrecks and wrecking there were problems for the Customs.

On 13th October 1738 (a Friday no less!) the *Bedra*, bound from Ireland to Ilfracombe, went ashore at Saunton Sands. Its cargo was estimated as 1,300 pounds of soap and candles – more items liable to a very high Excise duty. The Captain and his crew were quite determined that 'they had sooner the sea or the Country people have it [the cargo] than the Customs officer' and so they came to an agreement with the locals to share the spoils. However, the Captain's dealings with the wreckers backfired and he complained to the Collector at Barnstaple, who gathered a party of officers to search the area. Not one candle or one bar of soap was found, which is not really surprising as they were goods that could be easily hidden. The Captain had quite a bit of explaining to do and the case dragged on for several years before it finally petered out with no real conclusion.

Less than 30 years later, a brig became stranded on Woolacombe Sands – now a flourishing holiday centre, but then it was a rather desolate spot with just a few isolated farms. The riding officer, Mr Wright, did manage to secure 40 casks of brandy, which he had found in 'the cellar of a house used by the Lord of the Manor for the purpose of putting wrecked goods for safety'. A Customs guard was placed on the vessel but despite this more casks disappeared. One was found in a hedge some distance from the shore and when a full search of the area was undertaken three casks were found 'buried to a considerable depth under the Ground in a Public Plot adjoining the village'.

Then in July 1765 the Collector had a more dismal report to convey to the Customs Board in London. One of the Board's new cutters had come ashore at Woolacombe. The cutter was 'Twenty-three feet by the keel, supposed to have been built at Deal . . . calculated for the more speedie and easie coming at and boarding smuggling vessels. She is almost new but has received some damage to her bows as she was driven ashore.' Although the Collector did not name the vessel, from his description it would appear to fit the *Severn*, which was destined to serve for a number of years yet at Bristol so the damage it sustained could not have been too dramatic.

During the first part of the 18th century Barnstaple was an important port – fifth in the Kingdom. It boasted a good trade with

Spain, Portugal, France, Ireland, Newfoundland and most especially the American colonies. During the ten years between 1721 and 1731 over five million pounds of tobacco was imported, much of it for re-export to France and Spain though it is open to speculation just how much of this tobacco ultimately arrived at its foreign destination.

However, in 1737, the Collector at Barnstaple was quite complacent about smuggling. He considered it to be 'at a stand still and which we cannot but ascribe to ye good effects of late Acts'. He was apparently referring to the Act of Indemnity, which was passed in 1736. This Act, amongst other measures, brought in the death penalty for wounding Revenue officers and hard labour for those caught and convicted of unloading goods, or indeed making warning signals. He did, however, feel that 'the seamen on tobacco shipps throw all their loose tobacco brought home in pricks and twists to small vessels to run on ye coasts . . . some of this tobacco may be dryed and sold especially on its swimming soon on shore before ye saltwater has penetrated it . . .'

A mere ten years later the situation had drastically changed and the Collector was forced to report 'with great regret' that 'the smuggling trade on this coast is again begin'. It was his information that several vessels had run brandy and claret onto the coasts and that 'the pernicious trade will again be carried on with great impunity unless a smack be provided as ordered to prevent it.' The perennial plea of all Bristol Channel collectors would once again fall on deaf ears in London. In 1747 a 'large Irish wherry' was seen to unload quantities of brandy, tobacco and soap off Braunton Burrows. This large expanse of dunes, the longest and widest sands along the southern coast of the Channel, would seem a perfect spot for smuggling. The riding officer at Braunton, Joseph Mellor, recovered only three casks of brandy from this consignment, these were found hidden in the dunes. He made the point to his Collector that the area was so wild and the people so opposed to the Customs that it was impossible to patrol the area properly, 'nothing short of a troop of militia riding regularly will oppose the trade'.

Over the next 50 years there are frequent references in the Customs records to 'informations of landings of smuggled goods' in the area but only the odd cask of spirits was ever recovered. And across the river Taw at Instow, the tide-waiter spent many fruitless days searching the dunes to the north of the village for goods that had been landed (or so he had been 'credibly informed'). The locals must have greatly enjoyed the time-consuming but abortive efforts of the Customs and I have no doubt that the odd cask was left abandoned just to keep the Revenue men interested – a game of hide and seek played on a grand scale!

Instow Quay, where there was a Customs warehouse, was ideally situated, being at the confluence of the rivers Taw and Torridge. It developed during the 19th century from a small fishing village of no more than a cluster of cottages along a sandy beach into a rather elegant seaside resort. There was just one isolated Customs success at Instow when, in 1783, the land-waiter at Appledore (just across the river) seized 210 casks of spirits and 'much tobacco' at Jewel's Pill – not more than a stone's throw from Instow Quay. The seizure had been made from the *Maria*, a vessel bound for Barnstaple from Ireland, and it caused quite a local furore. Appledore was then in the Bideford collection and Jewel's Pill was at the utmost limits of the port of Barnstaple. The wranglings and arguments continued for some months and they were finally resolved by London, who decided quite wisely that the seizure reward (a not inconsiderable sum) should be shared equally between the two collections; this was despite the fact that Thomas Drake, the Appledore officer, had strongly implied that George Wackrill, the Instow officer, had countenanced the landing. Wackrill had previously been in hot water with his Collector for being absent from duty when goods were being deposited in the warehouse. With such internal squabbles, which can be mirrored elsewhere in the country, it is not really so surprising to note the Customs' dismal record against smuggling in the area.

There was, and had been for many years, a sharp rivalry between the two adjacent ports – Barnstaple and Bideford. Both were long-established and Bideford is now eternally remembered from the very start of Kingsley's book *Westward Ho* as 'the little white town which slopes upward from its broad tide river'. It had managed to stay ahead of its near neighbour, at least in trade terms, during the early decades of the 18th century. Bideford was then second only to London as far as tobacco imports were concerned and the port had a long and fine tradition of shipbuilding, which went back to the days of Grenville. In the 1720s Defoe commented on 'its considerable and wealthy merchants, who trade to most of the trading world'. It was from one of these merchant families that sprang the most notorious and certainly most audacious Channel smuggler – Thomas Benson.

The Benson family fortunes were founded on trade with the American colonies and, to a lesser extent, France and Portugal and when Thomas inherited the family business in 1743 he not only gained control of a fleet of a dozen vessels but also took possession of the family seat near Northam – Knapp House. Benson, through

123

influential contacts in London, managed to obtain privateering licences for his vessels. Though profitable at first these operations became rather expensive. However, in 1746, he was made Sheriff of Devon and one year later elected as Member of Parliament for Barnstaple. Due to his influence in London he obtained the contract to ship convicts out to the penal colonies in America at £20 per head and return with tobacco; it would appear to be a most profitable venture and one to restore his ailing fortunes.

In 1748 Benson obtained the lease of Lundy Island and soon he was landing his convicts there to work for him. His view was quite simple, 'it matters not where they were sent as long as it was out of the country'. But soon there were reports that the convicts were just a part of a more grandiose plan. The Custom Board in London reported to the Collectors at Barnstaple and Bideford that they had received evidence,

'. . . that a new trade is carried on at the Island of Lundy and that many ships bound outwards from Barnstaple Bay unload there and the cargoes are afterwards returned to that country in other vessels. That a platform with guns is erected and shot fired to bring ships to give an account of themselves who and what they are, but the men in them are not offered to land and it is apprehended unless an immediate stop be put to it, the island will become a magazine for smugglers . . .'

And what were the Collectors' responses to this new smuggling threat right on their doorsteps? Both replied that 'a smuggling trade may be carried on there if attempted with a great deal of success as a number of small vessels may constantly hover with safety in Lundy Road and there both land and take in goods in a clandestine manner to the great detriment of the Revenue'. They both admitted that they did not know how the illegal trade could be prevented because the island was not included in any of the Smuggling Acts, it was outside the bounds of the Kingdom and as such did not come within the limits of either port. However, they did feel it necessary to issue strict instructions to their officers 'to be alert to the considerable smuggling trade carryed on the coasts from Lundy'. At least the Board in London could not say that they had ignored the warning!

However, the Board decided to take the matter into their own hands; they served writs on Benson for several cargoes of tobacco that his vessels had loaded for export. These writs were, in effect, for repayment of the Customs duties that had been remitted to Benson. The Board were making the assumption that the tobacco had been smuggled back onto the mainland. The figures were quite staggering

– nearly 200,000 pounds of tobacco amounting to over £8,300 in duty, and there is no doubt that this was merely the tip of the iceberg as far as Benson's smuggling operations were concerned.

Benson decided to test the legality of the writs in the Courts – indeed on the face of it he appeared to have a reasonable case as there was very little evidence to support the Board's allegations. Meanwhile Benson had another scheme to improve his fortunes. In July 1752 he heavily insured his vessel the *Nightingale* and its cargo, which was loaded in Barnstaple. Within a day or so of leaving port the cargo was landed on Lundy. The vessel, with a skeleton crew and some convicts, sailed some 50 miles west of Lundy where it was fired and scuttled; the master and the crew took to the boats and finally landed safely at Clovelly. Benson, of course, claimed the insurance.

Almost two years later one of the crew was persuaded to turn King's evidence and he revealed the full details of the fraud. Benson knew that the game was finally up, especially as he had lost the judgement on his Court cases. He managed to escape the country leaving the master and the mate of the *Nightingale* to face the music. The mate was found not guilty but the master was convicted and was executed in 1754. Benson continued to trade successfully from Portugal until his death in 1771. It will never be possible to even estimate the amount of goods that Benson smuggled during his short reign at Lundy and but for his foolish fraudulent act he probably could have continued smuggling for many years. He had so fortified Lundy that it would have taken a military and naval operation to have prised him from his stronghold.

Benson was not the first, not indeed the last person to use Lundy Island as a safe haven for illegal operations. The island had long been a refuge for pirates, who were a constant threat and danger to vessels using the Bristol Channel. During Tudor times Robert Hickes of Saltash, a well-known pirate and privateer (the terms were almost synonymous!) operated from there, followed closely by another Cornish pirate – John Peers of Padstow. But perhaps the most notorious was John Challice, who used the island as his base from 1574 to 1581. Even the pilot's notes for the Spanish Armada recorded that Lundy would make a good refuge!

In the following century a pirate named Salkeld crowned himself 'King of Lundy' and when he was finally driven away a variety of 'pirates and rovers' used the island as a base to attack shipping and raid the Channel coasts. These were a cosmopolitan lot and at various times Turkish, Algerine, French and Spanish adventurers held sway. In 1698 a Richard Fulford petitioned the Customs   125

Commissioners to be appointed coast-waiter on the island and although the Commissioners agreed that it was a place 'where considerable quantities of goods were run', they did not feel that a permanent officer was justified. In 1721 Richard Scores was the tenant farmer on Lundy, but because 'so many illegal practices were taking place' he was forced to leave. Certainly in 1723 a large consignment of tobacco and spirits was seized on the island by the Barnstaple Customs; the crew of the preventive boat had actually rowed out to the island – quite a formidable feat. One of the crew was left on the island for two days to guard the seized cargo whilst the boat returned to port to arrange a suitable vessel to collect it.

After Benson's short reign, the lease was purchased by Sir John Borlase Warren, another Member of Parliament, who set about further strengthening the island's defences. In July 1776 the Barnstaple Collector reported that cannons, mortars, muskets, pistols and a considerable quantity of shot, shells and gunpowder had been loaded for the island, enough he vouchsafed to 'sustain a long siege'. As if confirmation was needed that Lundy was still being used for smuggling, Captain Dickinson of the armed brig *Lady Mackworth*, made a report to the Swansea Collector in November 1782. His vessel had been 'in the neighbourhood of Lundy' when he had sighted a small cutter off the island which he supposed was either a smuggler or a privateer. He immediately gave chase but was unable to come up close. Thereupon he manned two boats and sent them ashore to search the island; 'after they had landed they made a strict search, they found in the cavities of the rocks and in small huts 128 ankers of brandy and 4 bags of Bohea tea.' The Collector confirmed that it was his opinion that there was a very considerable trade carried on 'in the smuggling line on the said Island'.

As we will see later Thomas Knight, one of the most famous Channel smugglers, when driven from Barry Island in 1785 was thought to have merely moved his operation to Lundy. During the last decades of the 18th century the island was owned by John Cleveland, who leased it out to 'various tenants' under his supervision – no doubt all were involved in the Trade. Perhaps the last word on the island should be left with the Cardiff Collector, who maintained that 'there never lived yet a man on the island of Lundy who was not connected with smuggling'!

Appledore has a maritime lineage as long as any other Channel port. In 1350, John Toky, who was the Customs Collector for 'Barnstaple, Bydeforde, Ilfridecombe, Dunstore and Tawmouth' (the latter being the old name for Appledore), recorded a busy trade in wool and woolfells from the ancient port. Jan Morris, that incomparable travel writer, considers it to be 'the most absolutely maritime community in the British Isles' – an opinion difficult to contradict when one considers its small but delightful Custom House, its maritime museum, its lifeboat station, its shipyards and the few remaining mariners' houses that grace the many small 'opes' that lead up and away from the quay. Indeed the whole town seems to live and breathe its maritime past and present, not forgetting, of course, its smuggling traditions. Even in the 19th century its inhabitants were considered 'wild and uncivilised' and it is from this port that Benson planned many of his operations – he built a new quay in 1745.

Like so many places on the south coast of the Channel the town's reputation for smuggling cannot be justified on hard evidence; indeed there are precious few recorded seizures of any consequence. The Customs records may hint darkly at the extent of the illegal trade in the area but they have little to offer by way of facts. Perhaps the port's mariners preferred to operate their smuggling trade 'away from Home', as there are several instances of Appledore vessels being involved in the trade on other parts of the coast.

In 1752 the Naval vessel *Despatch*, which was temporarily seconded to the Collector at Barnstaple, was anchored at Quay Pool, Appledore. Captain Veal ordered his men to search the sloop *Boston*, which had just sailed in on the tide. The seamen found 13 ankers of rum and some lengths of linen and lawn hidden under the cargo of culm. A day later William Swayne, the tide-surveyor at the port, instigated his own rummage of the vessel and he found 'a further jarr and nine bottles of rum'. As the vessel had come from Neath just across the Channel, it is open to conjecture where they obtained the rum. Swayne thought that it had been obtained from an incoming Bristol vessel; as he put it 'there is a great concourse of vessels around the Island' – of course he meant Lundy!

Almost a decade later there was a replica seizure when the tide-waiter decided to search the *Nottage*, which had arrived from the port of Swansea. Two ankers of brandy were discovered in the master's cabin and later six small bales of tobacco and some bottles of wine were dug out of the coal. The Collector was caused to comment to London, 'these colliers are a great annoyance and cause continual problems. The fines for smuggling are not sufficient to put a stop to their business so much so that they dare risk a venture on every voyage.' Thomas Morris of the *Nottage* had been fined £20 and did not lose his vessel. On being pressed to disclose how and where he had obtained the goods, he reluctantly admitted that he had called in at Lundy and left the impression that the island was like a shop or supermarket for all manner of duty-free goods.

However, for most of the time the Customs at Appledore seemed to be involved in a wild goose chase around the Burrows. The Burrows are at Northam, now a country park and protected from the sea by a pebble ridge. Frequently the Customs spent many a long day searching the sands for goods that they had heard had been landed, but rarely finding any evidence. It was here in 1782 that the Revenue cutter *Scorpion* seized 50 ankers of brandy, 150 pounds of tobacco and four bags of tea; the goods had been landed from a Cornish smack, the *Lady Mary*, that regularly traded from the North Cornish ports and Bristol. Most of the cargo was secured from the beach but the Commander felt that an extended search was a waste of time because 'the local people are well versed in the trade'.

Wrecks were fairly frequent along the stretch of coast. For instance in 1791 a Fowey vessel, the *Abeona*, was stranded near Northam after it had landed a fair consignment of spirits, tea, tobacco and playing cards. One of the Barnstaple Excise officers, who seemed to be the only Revenue officer on hand, took possession of the spirits and tea. No mention is made of either the tobacco or playing cards. This is the first recorded instance of playing cards being smuggled in the Bristol Channel – though in truth they were rarely smuggled elsewhere. This fact is quite surprising as playing cards were a luxury item for all of the 18th century, due in no small measure to a prohibitive Customs duty *and* a high Excise duty. Perhaps the answer was that there was no ready market for cards, as most gaming houses were situated in London and the other large cities.

In October 1804 the Barnstaple Collector had the following to say about smuggling in the area:

'We find that smuggling in general has for some years been increasing and is carried on at present on the coast of Devon and Cornwall to an alarming Extent and in such a systematic manner that the Inhabitants of those Counties are regularly supplied with Smuggled spirits at a lesser price than they can be bought for at the public sales of condemned goods. The principal Places of landing on this side of the Channel are Clovelly (a place notorious for smuggling), Combe Martin, Lee and Lynmouth within the port of Ilfracombe . . .'

In the same report the collector 'deemed it necessary' to inform the Customs Board of 'the total incompetency of John Berry, Riding Officer at Clovelly, who was appointed to guard the coast from thence to Bude. He is exceedingly infirm being upwards of 70 years and we understand that he has not been on horseback for 20 years past'! Indeed a fair percentage of riding officers were over 60 years of age – so much for their romantic image! Considering that much of their work was physically demanding with the requirement to be out patrolling in all weathers, both day and night, very few of them were fit enough for the rigours and dangers of such an arduous life; all this for a meagre salary of £60 per annum.

The Collector mentioned Clovelly as a place notorious for smuggling and yet, search as one may, there are no recorded seizures in the vicinity until the early years of the 19th century. Its very isolation must have ensured its exclusivity as a favourite and safe landing place and it is favoured by being the only sheltered harbour along the coast – said to be the most dangerous and inhospitable stretch in the whole of the country. With riding officers of the calibre of Berry, Clovelly must have become a virtual 'free port' for most of the smuggling period. It seems highly likely that Benson used it as a regular landing place as it is but a short landfall from Lundy. Some of the caves off Hobby Drive, the splendid three mile walk that wends along the cliff tops, were said to have been stores for contraband cargoes. One cave to the east of the harbour still retains the name of 'Smugglers' Cave'.

Clovelly was discovered by the tourists of the 19th century and they came in their hordes on paddle steamers from Ilfracombe. The popularity of this unique village owes much to Charles Kingsley, who featured it in his writings, especially *Westward Ho*. Though Dickens also had a hand in it, he called it 'a mighty singular place and pretty place, I saw in all the days of my life.' Even today it still looks like the place where 'old-time smuggling' would have abounded.

During March 1805 the Revenue cutter *Shark*, which was then based at Padstow, seized a large 72 ton lugger, the *Dart* of Fowey, just off the harbour at Clovelly. The cargo of spirits, tobacco and pepper (obviously obtained from an East Indiaman) was taken to Padstow for auction. The seized vessel was condemned and brought into the Customs service. It was re-named *Busy* and served for several years on the south coast before ending its days as a quarantine boat. At this period vessels were at a premium and many Revenue cutters had been seconded to Naval duties.

Hartland Point, with Lundy Island about twelve miles due north, marks the extremity of the Bristol Channel coast. From this majestic headland the coast falls almost due south and faces the wild expanse of ocean, with the Atlantic rollers ceaselessly battering its rugged 129

Idealised versions of the smugglers' lives.

shore. It is from this stretch of the coast that comes the most famous smuggling legend of the West Country – John Copinger alias 'Cruel Copinger'.

The reputation, if it can be so styled, of this smuggler owes much to the writings of Rev. R. S. Hawker, that strange and rather eccentric clergyman who was appointed to the parish of Morwenstow in 1834. A time, it must be said, when smuggling had passed its peak. It is fair to say that Hawker tended to be a little economical with the truth and few of his stories can be backed by hard facts. However, he managed to weave and fabricate a quite frightening tale of an evil character that would put most real-life smugglers to shame.

According to Hawker, Copinger was said to have been of Danish origin, who first appeared off Hartland during a terrible storm when he was the only survivor of a wreck. He married a local girl – an heiress to boot – and then proceeded to set up a gang of desperate ruffians ready to turn their hand to any illegal activity – poaching, wrecking and smuggling. The coast from Hartland to Morwenstow, some five miles or so, is littered with caves and places said to be associated with Copinger. He was reputed to have cut off the hand of an Exciseman who was foolish enough to interfere in his activities and the local people lived in fear of him and his gang; Copinger appeared to treat harshly anybody who got in his way. He is said to have disappeared in just as mysterious a way as he arrived – he left by boat from Hartland to the accompaniment of thunder and lightning. He sailed into the storm and nothing more is heard of him, but he left behind this strong and lasting legend.

Very few facts can be positively established. Most importantly his name does not figure in any Customs records, which considering the reputed size of his smuggling operations is somewhat surprising. In 1792 a Daniel Herbert Coppinger survived a shipwreck at Marsland Mouth, just north of Morwenstow, and he did indeed marry a local heiress. However, he is shown on his marriage certificate as a member of the Navy. This Coppinger was made bankrupt in 1802 and he spent some time in prison as a result of an unpaid debt; this could have been on account of a smuggling offence. Coppinger is believed to have lived peacefully in Barnstaple after his release from prison.

A further complication to the story is that there was indeed a 'John Coppinger' who was active in smuggling in the latter decades of the 18th century. This Coppinger was a smuggling merchant of some importance, who operated from Port Rush in Ireland and more especially from Roscoff. It is quite possible that this Coppinger could have used his own smuggling vessels, though he was primarily known as a supplier of goods to other smuggling masters.

Hawker maintained that the Copinger legend was remembered in a 'ballad in existence within *living memory*' and of which only one verse had survived:

'Would you hear of "cruel" Copinger
He came from a foreign land;
He was brought by the salt water
And was taken away by the wind.'

Despite the fact that there is virtually no evidence to support the 'Cruel Copinger' legend, such stories cannot be dismissed out of hand; as we have seen elsewhere there is no smoke without fire. Smuggling by its very nature was, and is, a very secretive activity and many of its perpetrators gained heroic reputations in their own lifetimes. So it is not really surprising that their activities should become further embellished and exaggerated as they pass into folk-lore, making it nigh on impossible to distinguish fact from fiction. However, in the case of Cruel Copinger the myth has grown from no substantial evidence and one would doubt his very existence.

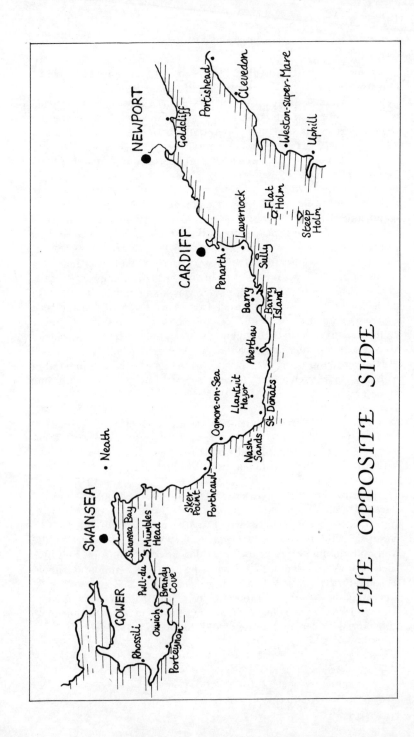

THE OPPOSITE SIDE

6
The Opposite Side

Most Englishmen would consider the Bristol Channel as *their* waterway and certainly its name implies some proprietary right to this claim. Most Welshmen would counter that its proper name is the Severn Sea and after all that river has its origin deep in the heartland of Wales. Whatever are the niceties of such a debate, I have taken 'the Opposite Shore' to describe the Welsh coast of the Channel from Chepstow to the Gower. Indeed no study of smuggling in the area would be complete without recalling the many incidents that occurred along this coast.

There are several natural factors that had an influence on this coast being specially favoured by many smugglers. Firstly, the fast flowing tide moves up the Channel in a north-easterly direction and this fact of nature coupled with the prevailing south-westerly winds makes this coast the easiest and most natural landing place in the Bristol Channel. The number of sailing vessels that were wrecked along the coast from the Gower to Aberthaw shows what powerful factors they were. Furthermore the Welsh coast is blessed with longer areas of open beach and sand dunes and generally has a less terrifying aspect than the North Devon coast. The Gower coast is lined with snug, sandy bays naturally designed for smuggling.

This stretch of coast had a long and established propensity for smuggling, as well as a notoriety for wrecking. The 'country people', as one Customs collector called them, gathered at a wreck in great numbers and plundered the cargo with a rare enthusiasm and they were quite prepared to (and frequently did) use force to retain their ill-gotten goods. Therefore the country people were pre-conditioned to illegal activities and they proved to be a ready and eager market for the 18th century smugglers.

They were, of course, all Welsh speaking and not only did they feel a certain kinship with the Irish smugglers but also considered smuggling a lawful and natural act against the penal duties imposed by a 'foreign' government. Another point to be borne in mind is that as they were Welsh-speaking there was far less likelihood of information on smuggling runs being passed on to the Customs authorities. 133

Indeed generally in the Bristol Channel very little information came to the Customs by way of the local people, unlike other areas where informants could be found providing the price was right.

The earliest references to smuggling along this coast relate to Chepstow. For centuries the Marcher Lords had ruled the area with little, interference from the monarchs. Amongst the ancient rights they claimed was freedom from Customs duties, and more especially exemption from prisage duty – the earliest duty on wines. Indeed for many centuries Chepstow operated almost as a free-port.

The port was under the control of the Bristol Customs and the Collector was frequently remonstrated with about the amount of smuggling at Chepstow. When he did send officers across in an attempt to suppress the trade, the local lords and merchants complained bitterly to the King about 'the outrageous actions of the customers arresting our rightful goods'. It was not until Tudor times, when the Customs administration was reorganised and established nationwide that the port produced and Customs revenue.

During the 16th century the Gower was a hotbed of smuggling, largely organised by the local gentry. The Mansell and Herbert families held sway for many years, often in opposition to each other, which frequently led to fights between the rival factions. John Lucas and his successors operated a smuggling empire from a large fortified house called 'Salthouse', which was situated near Port Eynon bay. Further east up the Channel, the Vaughan family of Dunraven Castle (near Southerdown) produced several generations of smugglers-cum-pirates – in the Bristol Channel the two activities seemed to be equally interchangeable! The Stradling family owned St Donat's Castle (now the famous Atlantic College) close to Nash Point and the notorious Nash Sands. This family had its own vessels, which regularly traded to France and were not averse to the odd spot of piracy.

Penarth Road, or 'Penhearthe rode before Cardiffe' as it appears in the Elizabethan State Papers, was a familiar and favourite spot for both smugglers and pirates alike. It was one of the few safe havens for vessels along that stretch of coast. In 1575 it was reported that 'the Townsmen of Cardiffe and sundry gentlemen there abouts do commonly buy and receive divers of the goodes and spoiles brought thither by Callis [a well-known Lundy pirate] and his complices, and give them aide with victualles and other necessaries'.

During the 1640/50s the Customs Collector at Cardiff was a certain John Byrd and he obligingly left some brief notes on smuggling in his port. He lived in Caerleon, some 15 miles from the main port, although Caerleon was then a busy trading port shipping farm produce to Bristol. On 7th September 1649 Byrd wrote:

'seized on 34 great rowles and 14 hand rowles of Barbadoes tobaccoe, which was privately landed at Redwick [six to seven miles east of Newport]. The tobaccoe was about 2,000 lb weight, which was the goods of Thomas Northerne, Sam Roche, Wm. Turkey and others of the shipp *Elizabeth and Ann* of Bristoll and it was landed with an intente to defraude the state of Customs & Excise.'

This is the first ever written evidence of the smuggling of goods liable to Excise duty – the Excise duty had only been introduced in 1643.

A year or so later Byrd received information from London that a Bristol vessel, the *North Starr*, was to land smuggled tobacco at Newport. However, Byrd and his deputy at Newport examined every 'vessell and caske' but found that they contained 'only pruens, which were genearally conceived to bee tobaccoe'. Six months later the information from London was more reliable, as he seized some 'caskes of Mollasses were in facto Brandies'.

The troubles in Ireland during 1688–90 resulted in an embargo on all Bristol Channel shipping to and from Ireland. This prohibition put a great premium on smuggling, especially considering the large Irish trade to and from the Channel ports. The Customs Board in London were for once aware of the dangers and in February 1690 issued an instruction to all the Customs collectors in the Channel ports; it provides a fitting introduction to the new era of smuggling.

'The late Act prohibiting all trade and Commerce with France and Ireland has occasioned great art and Industry to be used in Carying on the Smuggling trade and privattie stealing on shore. Both prohibited and unCustomed goods to the great hindrance and prejudice of their Majesties Reveniew of Customs. . . . you and all the officers of your port are to quicken greater diligence in looking out for the preventing of fraudes in this Kinde and you are all to take Notice that if wee shall hereafter know of any goods Rune with the lymits of your port we shall account itt as the Neglect of your selves and the other officers and proceed against you.'

Strong words and fine sentiments, no doubt, but they were quickly overtaken by a vast escalation of smuggling in the next century.

Little is heard on the smuggling front until the 1730s, when suddenly it burst forth like a forest fire. In February 1732 the Cardiff collector made the first of many pleas to London to provide 'a sloop to patrol the Channel'. He suggested that it should be 'built plain without any painting or ornament, nor any Colours to be put out'.

He felt that in this way the smugglers would be apprehensive of every sloop they saw coming close to them. In order to support his case the Collector reported that 'the Smugglers do begin in this Channel to appear and about a fortnight ago there was one of them off Aberthaw & Barry, but as no boat did Venture out to her as they were too strong a force.' A small Naval sloop called the *Hawke* was provided but as it had to patrol from Milford to King's Road (Portishead) it was not particularly effective and was soon removed. It had not made any seizures, and thus it was deemed that there was no smuggling in the area!

In these early days it is quite amazing the amount of detailed information that was supplied from London on smuggling runs in the Channel. Vessels from Bridgwater carrying 'hillingstones' (roofing tiles) were strongly suspected of carrying tobacco and rum to Newport, Cardiff and Aberthaw. The notoriety of the Bristol Channel pilots had filtered through to London, 'you are to bee warned that everie pilote is a venturer'! However, the first recorded seizure at Aberthaw was 14 pounds of human hair; this rather grotesque item was found hidden under cargo on one of the regular market boats that traded with Bristol. A year later the warehouse at the small port was broken into and six casks of brandy were stolen. William Roberts, who was the sole officer at the port, suspected that the 'Armed Gang at Sully' were responsible. Sully Island is almost four miles south of Penarth, just off Lavernock Point. It can be reached by foot during the ebb tide and as its name suggests it was first inhabited by the Vikings. Roberts said that he needed a boat and the assistance of the military before he dare set foot on the island, and as he received neither, nor indeed was he armed, he wisely did not venture forth!

In 1734 the Cardiff Collector felt it necessary to acquaint the Customs Board in London with the state of smuggling in his area. His report throws much light on the smuggling methods of the time.

'At Aberthaw and Barry when any boats goes out to em from thence, the Owners of em have always a Spye on the officer; and when they find him on one side of the river at Aberthaw, they'll land what they have on the other; and by reason there is no boat in the Service, nor any boat on those acco'ts to be had for love nor money, and the officer is obliged to go to a bridge about two miles round, they have time enough to secure the goods before he can get there. Nay, there is instances that they'd run'd goods in the day time before the Officer's face in this Manner. At Barry tis the same case; if they find the officer on the Iseland they'll land the other side of the Harbour. If the other side of the Harbour they'll land on the Iseland and the officers can't get over till the Tide is out, wch may be five or six hours; and there is so much cover on the Iseland, and such conveniencys for hiding of goods the other side, that an officer Has but a poor Chance to meet with em after they are landed. At Ogmore River it is the same and so at Aberavon.'

It sounds like a harmless game of hide and seek but on a grand scale!

If the Collector had his problems near at hand on his coast, he must have been dismayed to receive regular messages from London about 'the running of goods on a small island called Flat Holms within the Bristol Channel'. Flat Holm, though situated not far off the Somerset coast, was actually under the control of the Cardiff Customs. It had long been considered part of Wales and its Welsh name was 'Ynys Hafren' or the Isle of the Severn. It was also the natural home of the wild leek – the national emblem of Wales. In 1735 he was clearly instructed by London that the Customs boat at Cardiff should regularly patrol the island to 'prevent any fraudes'. London's information, and one wonders as to its source, was that goods were landed on the island during the day and then distributed at night onto both sides of the Channel.

The smugglers who were using Flat Holm were Richard Robinson and his son, Pasco. The father's vessel was over 80 tons and the son's a smaller sloop of 40 tons. Certainly Pasco did not believe in anonymity, his sloop was said to have been painted a brilliant red with a mermaid as a figurehead. The Robinson's obtained their tea, tobacco and brandy from Guernsey and the journey time from home base to the Channel must have taken at least a week even in the most favourable weather conditions, so it is not really surprising that London were able to inform Cardiff of the Robinsons' arrival. Despite having these advance warnings neither father nor son were ever captured. It is believed that they retired wealthy men and masterminded smuggling operations from Guernsey to South and South-West England.

Perhaps as a result of the depressing and dismal reports they were receiving about smuggling in the Cardiff area, the Customs Board sent one of its top men to inspect the port to appraise the situation at first hand. Thomas Ja'ns, the Surveyor-General, arrived late in 1736 and his report merely confirmed that smuggling in the area had reached a desperate state. According to him Barry Island was 'a most hazardous district over-run by ruffians', at Aberthaw he found that 'the running of goods on the coast was quite commonplace' and the guard at Cardiff 'was non-existent'. Newport and the river Usk 'where the tides were very strong' was open to all vessels and none had been searched within memory. Ja'ns had some particularly

137

forceful and pertinent observations on the various officers at the port and their 'sad lack of urgency in their business'. One was 'old and infirm', another 'spent more time in the tavern', and the officer at Barry 'was most lax in her Majesty's service'! He left the collector in no uncertainty as to his opinions and gave him detailed instructions on the proper rummaging (searching) of vessels, which were to be copied to every member of staff.

These instructions are really quite amazing as they detailed the various contrivances used on vessels to conceal smuggled goods – false bulkheads and decks, compartments hollowed out of cabins, hollow masts and other hiding places. He also gave clear directions as to the proper use of spits to search cargo and ballast for hidden goods. Most writers on smuggling have attributed such smuggling devices to a so-called 'scientific period of smuggling' dating from 1820 onwards; and yet almost 100 years earlier there is evidence that such methods were well-known and presumably well-used even then.

Whether as a result of his inspection and shake-up, the seizure record of the port improved during the next few years – though experience shows the more likely answer was that smuggling itself had further increased. In a very rare combined operation, the local officer at Aberthaw and the local Excise officer patiently watched a vessel hovering off the coast at Sully. Their forebearance was rewarded, as they witnessed casks being landed before the vessel made off in the direction of Barry. The Customs man commandeered a boat to give chase to the smuggling vessel but alas to no avail. The Excise officer followed the smugglers on horseback with a little more success. He was able to seize four casks of brandy and detain just one smuggler. It did seem a poor reward for all the effort, especially as 'Thomas Issack', the captured smuggler, was considered 'an idiot, who did not understand what he was doing' by the local jury and allowed to go scot-free. It sounds a most contrived story, with Issack as a deliberate scapegoat. It was impossible to obtain a smuggling conviction in prosecution cases because of the bias of the local magistrates and juries.

In 1738 at Penarth the local Customs men seized tobacco and rum from a small coasting vessel from Bristol that 'uses no other trade than to carry culme for burning of lime and stones to the Sea Wall'. The two Customs boatmen boarded the vessel at dawn and they felt that the smuggled goods belonged to 'a man of substance named Edwards, who had lately Built a house by the Harbour where there was never one before [Penarth became a most fashionable residential town for Cardiff in the late Victorian age] . . . he is an old offender and it is reputed that he has built large cellars to store his goods'. They further felt that Edwards' sole reason for living in such a place 'was to defraud the Customs'. There was an added complication, the Customs moored their boat right by Edwards' house and he threatened to sink the vessel should the Customs interfere with his 'lawful business'. Other quantities of brandy were found on the shore at Penarth and it was assumed that they too were part of Edwards' cargo. Needless to add that no prosecution was brought against this 'man of substance'!

Not only did the Customs officers have to contend with smuggling but they also had the responsibility for the securing of wrecked goods. There are numerous wrecking incidents along this coast but one example will suffice to give the flavour of this illegal activity. In 1737 the *Pye*, a snow (three-masted vessel) bound for Bristol with tobacco, sugar and cotton, was wrecked off Nash Point and in next to no time, 'three to four hundred people from all parts of the Country towards the Hills' assembled on the beach to pillage the cargo and used considerable force to beat off the handful of Customs officers there to collect the cargo. Soldiers from Swansea were called out to arrest the worst gang 'from a little town called Bridgend, most of them shoomakers'. However, the military were not prepared to enter Bridgend unless each man received £20 reward – an enormous sum in those days. The military exercise did not take place because nobody could decide where the money would come from, as precious little cargo was saved.

Despite all this illegal activity, the Collector at Cardiff could calmly report to London, in 1740, that there was no truth in the rumour that large quantities of tea, tobacco and spirits were being *daily* run on their coasts. It was his opinion that 'since the recent Act the smugglers had made no attempt in his district'! He was referring to the Act of Indemnity, which provided a free pardon for all smugglers who confessed their past offences and, more importantly, disclosed the names of all their accomplices. In retrospect there is no evidence that this Act had any material effect on the smuggling trade, nor indeed did the other draconian Acts that followed year after year.

And yet barely three years after giving his port a clean bill of health, he is to be found pleading with the Board in London for his 'preventive officers' to be supplied with firearms. It was agreed that each would have 'a pair of pistols, a hanger and a short gun'. The Collector, himself, was given a brace of pistols 'made in Bond Street with a fine mechanism and well-balanced'. It is very unlikely that he ever fired these in anger, at the time he was aged 68 years and 'not given to patrolling', as one Inspector rather succinctly commented.

Irish soap and candles (both liable to a high Excise duty) were regularly seized from vessels taking coal to Dublin. Most of the seizures were found in the cargo and one consignment of soap was found concealed in a hide of leather, which was submerged in the water and dragged behind the vessel as it entered the river Taff. An early example of sinking cargo, which became a major part of the smuggling scene some 70 years later. The officer at Aberthaw detained 'two ladies who looked bigg with child', they had several pounds of soap concealed 'neath their garments'! However, it was the unanimous opinion of all the officers that the Channel pilots were all in the smuggling trade and nothing could prevent their dealings but 'a small sloop to cruise as far as Lundy to meet the incoming vessels and escort them up to King's Road', where it was felt that the Customs presence was strong enough to prevent any smuggling.

140   An early photograph of Newport, before the large dock development.

The only two vessels in the Channel during the mid century were two cutters of the quarantine service. These 'guard ships' were to ensure that no goods were landed or any crew escaped during the quarantine period. The appropriately named *Severn* was stationed at the mouth of the Avon and the *Lawton* at Swansea. Both occasionally cruised the Channel if there were no vessels to guard but there is no evidence of either of them ever making a seizure. What didn't help matters was that the two captains appeared to be sworn enemies and took every opportunity to cause trouble for one another. The original cause of their dispute was that they were rivals for the affection of a certain widowed lady, but they seemed more intent on damaging each other than bothering with the smugglers!

The problems the Collector at Cardiff had with the locals is graphically illustrated by his complaint of 'the many little tobacco shops in this country'. It was his considered opinion that they obtained all their supplies from the smugglers but was unable to prove it because the shopkeepers were 'ignorant and illiterate people that don't understand a word of English or so they would make you believe'! The Collector at Neath had earlier made a similar comment about 'the unruly Welsh colliers', who had 'a great thirst for rum and brandy' and this he felt was the main cause of smuggling on his coast. The Swansea Collector made almost the same accusations, he stoutly maintained that since 'a new colliery had been opened at Kidwelly' the smuggling in the area had increased dramatically.

The Gower coast was a constant nightmare for the Swansea officers. In 1759 a West Indiaman bound for Bristol calmly moored off Rhossili Bay and landed large quantities of rum, sugar and molasses in daylight. The officers could not get near the beach because there was 'a mobb of nigh on four hundred' who had assembled to carry off the goods. And at Newton (near Porthcawl) another Bristol vessel discharged quantities of sugar, coffee and cocoa, and as the local officer reported, 'the country people are quite outrageous and threaten our very lives'. The officer was asked why no rum had been landed and he replied that he had been reliably informed that it had been off-loaded near Mumbles Head as there was a better market for spirits at that place!

The port of Swansea was beset by troubles during the 18th century. There was continual friction between the Excise and Customs officers at the port. The main bone of contention was which service had the right to rummage a vessel first. London's view was that the first officers to board a vessel had gained the right to the first search. This decision pleased neither and one gains the impression that the Revenue officers were too busy squabbling amongst them- 141 selves to worry overmuch about smuggling. The Custom House at the port was broken into twice, the first time some seized tea and brandy was stolen and the second time over £90 was taken. Although rewards were offered no culprit was found. Some years later the Collector absconded with a large sum of money and was believed 'to be residing in France'! So it is not surprising that the seizure record of the port was dismal, to say the least.

Flat Holm was still a constant concern to the Cardiff officers. The Surveyor regularly took the Penarth boat to patrol round the island. Considering that this vessel was merely an 18 foot yawl manned by only two boatmen, each the wrong side of 50 years, and the Surveyor was 49 years, they and their vessel were no match for any smuggling vessel. However, in September 1757, whilst visiting Flat Holm, they found the *Warren*, a Bristol vessel from Antigua, hovering near the island. It all seemed highly suspicious, especially as 24 puncheons of rum, 30 casks of sugar and several bales of cotton were already on the deck as if just waiting to be landed. The master of the vessel was ashore on the island and, what was a greater concern, there were 'two pleasure vessels filled with gentlemen of this town [Cardiff] and Bristol at anchor close to the shore'. The Surveyor managed to persuade the pleasure vessels to leave and the master to sail on to Bristol; luckily no violence was offered. At least the presence of a Customs boat, however small, had prevented an illegal landing, although the Surveyor ruefully commented that once they had left the scene the vessels could easily return, and short of stationing an officer on the island nothing could be done to stop such trade. A sad postscript to this incident was that just a few years later the two boatmen – John Vincent and Thomas Williams – were both drowned when their yawl foundered in a squall off Penarth Head. It is a strange but bitter fact that the sea took a more savage toll of Revenue boatmen and seamen than the smugglers ever did, despite all their infamous violence.

It was often the case that when a collector unwisely commits to paper a statement that smuggling has decreased or ceased at his port, he quickly has to regret such rash comments. In June 1766 the Cardiff collector reported, 'our officers are so well stationed and so little escapes them that we find no attempt to run any goods and no seizure has been made here for a considerable time.' (Of course the two statements are not complementary.) Within twelve months he is forced to report (in some detail) the number of smuggling vessels suddenly using the coasts. Barely two years after the purchase of the Isle of Man comes the first mention of vessels arriving from Rush.

First and foremost was the cutter commanded by John Connor

(alias Jack the Bachelor), which mounted six carriage guns, swivels and small arms. The famous, or notorious, Jack was described as 'a low set squat fellow of about 35 years with a small stoppage in his speech'. Another Irish smuggler, Thomas Field, captained a large cutter with eight carriage guns; Field was said to be 'about 44 years – a wellset made fellow'. John Creemans ran an Irish wherry, and two brothers, Stephen and Thomas Richards, also used an Irish wherry and its crew were 'desparate ruffians'. Last, but certainly not least, came Thomas Knight, with a cutter and a Scotch wherry. He was described as a 'middle-sized fellow about the age of 36 years with a dark complexion and pitted face.' During the next 15 years Knight would create havoc for the Cardiff officers.

The Swansea Collector was no more circumspect in his writings. In 1776 he felt that 'although smuggling had greatly increased with ships from Ireland and there was a considerable trade on the Gower coasts, a *small* cutter to cruise from Tenby along this coast and the Bristol Chanell [sic] and on the English coast down as far as Bideford. A vessel with twelve men will be sufficient as no great force is required here and if commanded by an active man we make no doubt she would well answer the end of appointing her. There is at present no vessel stationed in the Bristol Chanell where a great number of foreign ships arrive and much smuggling business is done.' What utter faith or sheer blind ignorance to think that one small cutter could hope to compete with the plethora of Irish smuggling vessels that were now using the Channel.

The flood-gates had opened with a vengeance and over the next ten years, the Connors, the Richards and Knight appeared to land their cargoes with impunity and with a scant regard for the meagre number of Revenue officers opposing them. Barry Island and Sully were natural smuggling strongholds where no Customs man dared to go, and even Flat Holm was severely out of bounds to the Customs. The new Cardiff surveyor woefully commented, 'I darest not send the boat there for fear of the men's lives.' In any case the Penarth boat was 'now too old to go into any sea'! As if the Connors and Knight were not enough to contend with, the Collector was informed that a cutter called *The King of Prussia* was now operating in the Channel; this vessel was owned and operated by Henry Carter, the patriarch of the famous smuggling family. Life was no easier at Swansea, there the smuggling king was William Arthur. A combined Customs and Excise raid on his house in Gower, in 1788, resulted in the Revenue men being faced by 50 persons 'armed with pokers, iron-bars, large knives, loaded whips and other offensive weapons'. It was quite impossible to serve any writ on him. The   143

Customs asked for the assistance of the Army but were firmly told that 'the situation of forces at present will not admit any detachment being sent into South Wales.'

The successes against Knight were very few and far between. In 1782 a small smuggling vessel of a mere 18 tons was seized. The vessel was considered 'to be very well-built and will do Exceedingly well for a Custom House boat at Penarth, she is believed to belong to Knight's gang.' It had been damaged by striking the rocks at Breaksea Point, where it was abandoned by the crew on the appearance of the Customs. They also seized a horse loaded with two kegs of brandy.

The biggest seizure was made at Goldcliff near Newport, where nearly 10,000 pounds of 'finely cut tobacco' and 40 gallons of brandy were found in a barn not far from the shore. The farmer gave evidence that a band of armed men had forced him to hand over his building for their use. By his description of the leader, it was deduced that Knight was responsible. The tobacco was removed to Cardiff for storage and it had to be guarded by armed men 'as the country is at present full of smugglers and the People here are in such Dread of Knight and his gang'. Just two months later a large consignment of rum and brandy was discovered almost at the same spot. On each occasion the smugglers had made their escape. It is obvious that the seizures had been made on information supplied by the Excise officer at Barry, because for the next month the Excise officer petitioned for a share in the seizure reward – all to no avail, which certainly did not help inter-service harmony.

Thomas Hopkins, the Customs waiter and searcher at Barry, showed great courage in opposing Knight; lesser men would have turned a blind eye. Whilst Knight and his men were away in Ireland, Hopkins and his men landed on the island and seized a large consignment of wine. A fortnight later Hopkins reported that 'a large cutter is now off the Island of Barry, it has 24 guns and 35 men running goods on the said Island'. This was in 1784 when Hopkins could not 'conceive any body has any Business there, who is not connected with Knight in Smuggling.'

Today it is almost impossible to visualise Barry Island as an island because it is now so built-up and developed as a holiday complex. Yet in the late 18th century it was covered with trees and with ample places to hide smuggled goods. Furthermore it had a splendid beach, quite perfect for the landing of goods. Even a century later Barry was still a mere hamlet of 17 houses and less than 50 inhabitants. The massive development of the docks changed all that and within ten years Barry was the largest coal exporting port in the country. Barry Island lost its identity as an island in the early 20th century as it became *the* seaside resort for the teeming population of the Welsh valleys.

In February 1785 over one ton and a half of smuggled salt was seized on the island by the intrepid Hopkins. Perhaps this success spurred the Customs on to greater urgency, for in the following month the Customs and Excise officers made a joint effort to capture Knight. Unfortunately there are no details of the operation or indeed whether Knight made a fight of it; the collector merely reports that 'Trade [smuggling] was totally put to a stop by our driving him [Knight] from the Island, we consider he has with-drawn to Lundy'. There can be no doubt that Knight had had a very good innings, for virtually 20 years he had plagued the Cardiff Customs. He was now close to 55 years, getting a bit old for the cut and thrust of the smuggling trade. Perhaps he 'retired' to Lundy, because little is heard of him again.

However, the Customs had little time to bask in their victory. Within six months Arthur extended some of his operations to the 'vacant' island, though not for long before another smuggler stepped in – William Doggett. Doggett was the only smuggler in the area who seemed prepared to attack Customs officers. It was for this reason that the Collector pleaded for 'sixty men of light infantry' and an armed cutter to be stationed at Penarth. Unfortunately neither request was answered. If only the Customs Board had listened to the pleas the story might have been much different. They would have probably argued that compared with the smuggling around the south and east coasts the illegal trade in the Bristol Channel was relatively insignificant and not really worth the effort and expense – certainly their precious resources of men and vessels were at break-ing point trying to cope on other coasts. Yet when the *Endeavour*, a Customs cutter stationed at Milford for patrolling the Irish Sea, entered the Channel it invariably proved worthwhile. In December 1787 the cutter captured three smuggling vessels; two of them were merely 'smuggling yawls', but the third was a cutter called the *Two Friends*, with John Hammond as master. Hammond hailed from Guernsey and was known there as 'a well-known smuggler'. The vessel was loaded with 140 ankers of brandy and rum, 70 bales of tobacco and 40 bags of tea. It had been taken whilst hovering off Limpert Bay near Breaksea Point, without much of a fight. The Customs were of the firm belief that the cutter belonged to 'Knight of Lundy', if this was so it would appear that Knight had gone into the business of 'smuggling broker'.

Newport and the mouth of the river Usk seemed to be a favourite 145 spot for the trade. In 1791 Richard Burton (his real name!), the Newport boatman, attempted to board a skiff, which was acting suspiciously at the mouth of the river Ebbw. However, in his own words, 'the persons on bord with horrid imprecations recited me, swearing that if I presum to come on bord they w'd blow my brains out and at the same time brandising a cutlass and pointing a pistol with horrid threats on my life.' Burton reported that it was a brand new vessel with black sides and the upperworks painted red and the name painted on her stern was *John of Combe*. He said that the skiff was owned by William Brown, 'a desperate villain', who lived at Newport but also had a house on Barry Island. It is interesting to note that Burton, who was described as 'a stout lusty sailor', retired from the Customs and founded a shipping company that figured prominently in the affairs of both Newport and Bristol.

Barry Island still continued to be a problem to the Customs. In 1798 the Collector himself led a large party of officers to the island following information he had received from a local constable. They found 297 casks of brandy, 20 hampers and two boxes of 'bottled wine', which local rumour suggested had been landed from an 'American' ship that had recently left Bristol. The brandy had been found cleverly buried in sand-dunes. Two days later they returned to the island and discovered three chests of tea hidden in an outhouse. It was later confirmed that the brandy and wine had been loaded at Bristol duty-free for export barely two weeks earlier. This was the most successful operation ever conducted at Barry and it more than anything sealed the fate of the island as a smuggling haven.

As the century drew to a close the Cardiff Collector summed up the state of smuggling in the area.

'At Newport where three rivers empty themselves into the Channel the situation is very convenient for smuggling.being so well calculated to prevent pursuit and commodious for landing; the chief articles are brandy and geneva, which was thought to be carried into the interior on horseback and brought to the coast from Barry Island and Aberthaw. At Barry strong armed vessels from Ireland and France land spirits and salt and smuggling vessels use the safe harbour at Penarth because the force of our boat is not strong enough to counteract.'

Nothing had really changed over the previous century. Nevertheless the days of the smuggling gangs and large runs were fast drawing to a close.

At one place along the Welsh coast old-fashioned smuggling runs were still in favour and still proving very successful. This was the

Swansea Bay and The Gower were well known smuggling areas.

Gower. The appropriately named Brandy Cove and its near neigh-bour Pwll-du were the most popular smuggling bays, especially used by William Arthur and his gang. Even today the two bays are not easy to reach on foot; hauling the smuggled goods up the precipitous cliff-path must have been a difficult task. Though at the western end of Pwll-du Bay there are the ruins of a cottage halfway up the path, reputed to have been used by the smugglers as a meeting place. Once on the clifftop the goods were moved up the Bishopton valley and then along a lane (still called Smugglers Lane) to the two farms – Great and Little Highway – which were the centres of Arthur's smuggling empire.

However, the days of Arthur and his deputy, John Griffiths, were coming to a close. In April 1804 a Lieutenant Sawyers of the Sea Fencibles and Francis Bevan, a local Customs officer, were on patrol along Oxwich beach. The Sea Fencibles were almost a floating Home Guard, specially formed to guard against invasion. Their boats were specially licensed and they were allowed to carry arms. Along the south coast of England most members of the Fencibles were thought to be in the smuggling trade.

On this particular evening Sawyers and Bevan sighted a cutter entering the bay and come to anchor, whereupon two men in a boat landed on the beach and enquired the whereabouts of Highway! It seems quite unbelievable that this should happen and much to the 147 credit of Sawyers and Bevan they did not enquire further to avoid suspicion, but merely informed them that it was just round the next headland (Pwll-du Head).

The Sea Fencibles and other revenue officers were brought out to lay siege to the two farms. Both farms were thoroughly searched and the smuggled goods were finally found hidden under the floor of the kitchen and also in a barn. The night's haul came to 420 casks of spirits, amounting to nearly 3,000 gallons. However, not all the casks arrived at the Swansea Custom House. Bevan left some casks with a mob of about 200 country people who had gathered and were threatening to attack the officers. As Bevan explained, 'some of them were much intoxicated, very clamorous and troublesome, requesting that they be allowed to drink'. This was one of the biggest seizures in the Gower and it led directly to the break-up of Arthur and his gang. It was believed that Arthur retired to Devon where he had a large estate, no doubt financed by his 30 or so years of smuggling enterprise.

In the following year George Beynon, the Customs officer at Rhossili, along with a party of Sea Fencibles, surprised a gang landing goods in Rhossili Bay. The smugglers managed to make good their escape but they left the beach littered with over 100 casks of brandy, geneva and wines. Later in the same year another consignment of tobacco and spirits was seized in the same bay. Obviously the Sea Fencibles of the Gower were of a higher calibre and reputation than their counterparts elsewhere.

Just two years later, in 1807, another large seizure was made at Middleton, a village just inland at the southern end of Rhossili Bay. The goods – some 30 kegs of brandy and over 1,200 lbs of tobacco, were found hidden in a haystack. The tables had been turned on the smugglers, such successes heralded the demise of large-scale smuggling on the Gower. No operator could afford to lose such consignments and it was now very clear that the chances of successfully landing goods were becoming rather slim.

It was the establishment of the Preventive Waterguard in 1809/10 that had a positive effect on the decline of smuggling, especially in the Bristol Channel. This 'new' Waterguard's duty was to operate in coastal waters and to tackle the smugglers who had managed to evade the Customs vessels that operated further out to sea. When the weather was too rough to take out their small rowing boats, they were expected to patrol the coast on foot and act as a link with the riding officers.

The recruits to this new force were mainly selected from seamen discharged from the Navy, which was contracting as a direct result of its own success at the Battle of Trafalgar. Quite deliberately the men were stationed a long way from their homes – this was to avoid collusion with relations and friends who might be in the smuggling trade. Therefore living accommodation had to be found for the men and this proved to be a most difficult problem because of the opposition and hostility of the local people, who were not prepared to offer any help to the Customs service.

The new preventive stations were set up in notorious smuggling places and perhaps it is not surprising to find that one was established at Aberthaw. No suitable accommodation could be found in the area for 'the sitter' (the officer in charge) and his six boatmen. The collector was therefore forced to compulsorily purchase land to build a watch-house and boat shed. The men appointed to Aberthaw all came from Shoreham in Sussex and they arrived in July 1810. Until their watch-house was completed they were forced to live in tents under quite miserable conditions. The pay was not high, the boatmen received £5 per annum and 3s a day when employed and the sitter £15 and 4s a day. They were expected to make-up their pay with seizure rewards. Another preventive station was placed at Nottage (near Porthcawl) and one on the north coast of the Gower at Whitford.

Less than twelve months after the Preventive Service had been in operation the Cardiff Collector was able to report, '. . . we have reason to think that no smuggling has been carried on within the limits of this port.' At Swansea the message was, '. . . there is no smuggling of any magnitude'. Perhaps this time both officials were correct, because only very isolated instances of smuggling occur in the reports over the next ten years. Despite the Aberthaw boat (which had to be replaced twice due to both boats sinking in heavy seas), Barry Island still appeared to figure in smuggling. In 1818 a large cargo of spirits had been landed, the preventive men only managed to seize three kegs. It was reported that spirit dealers in Cardiff were selling smuggled brandy for as little as 16s a gallon. However, most of the spirits quickly disappeared into the canal barges to find their way to the ready markets of the coal mines and iron works of the Rhondda, Rhymney and Ebbw valleys. With the quite phenomenal growth of the ports of Swansea, Cardiff and Newport over the next 50 years, most of the smuggling was by way of the crews of vessels trading to these ports. Jack the Bachelor, the Robinsons and Thomas Knight were just names to conjure with and they were firmly in the past.

7

The Beginning of the End

By the beginning of the 19th century the Customs Service had been waging a desperate and bitter war against the smugglers lasting for nigh on 100 years. It had been a long and unremitting conflict, vicious and bloody at times, with very little respite and with most of the honours, if indeed they may be called such, falling to the smugglers. At certain periods all seemed lost and it almost appeared that the smugglers would swamp the hard-pressed and beleaguered authorities; Lord Pembroke's observation made in 1781, 'Will Washington take America, or the smugglers England first?', merely acknowledged the gravity of the situation at that time – and yet there was worse to come.

There can be no doubt that the brunt of the illegal trade and the fury and violence of its perpetrators was borne by the Customs officers serving along the south and east coasts of England and that the Bristol Channel officers escaped relatively unscathed. Here in the Channel there was no overt confrontation, no deaths or injuries were suffered at the hands of the smugglers. Perhaps the worst fate the officers had to endure was a certain loss of dignity and respect as they were continually fooled and outwitted by the free-traders and their local supporters. Galling though it may be, the Channel officers had to accept that for most of the period they were unable to compete on equal terms with the smuggler.

During one of the many Parliamentary debates on smuggling, a Lord expressed the view in 1805 that

'It is impossible totally to prevent smuggling; the interested motives of mankind will always prompt them to attempt it particularly when taxes are extremely high, and the hope of large profits is a temptation sufficient to make light of any risk; all that the legislature can do is to compromise with the crime which, whatever laws may be made to constitute it a high offence, the mind of man can never conceive as at all equalling in turpitude those acts which are breaches of clear moral virtues.'

Not a particularly encouraging outlook and one unlikely to raise the morale of those forces faced with the problem of defeating the smuggling trade.

However, by 1810, there were some indications, though still somewhat faint, that the worst of the battle was over and that maybe at long last the Customs Service was beginning to assert itself and stamp its authority along the coasts. The first encouraging sign was the slow but steady increase in the number of seizures of smuggled goods, though this fact taken in isolation could be misleading; it could mean on one hand that smuggling was increasing and that the Customs were merely getting the same share from a larger trade, or on the other hand it could demonstrate an improved performance by the officers. A more positive and significant indication was the successful introduction of the Preventive Waterguard. Although their early results were less than spectacular, they had provided a far greater Revenue presence along the coasts, which in itself produced a restraining influence on the smuggling trade. Their value purely as a preventive measure can never be properly assessed but nevertheless it should not be ignored or indeed under-estimated.

Certainly many Customs officials along the Bristol Channel coast felt that at long last the tide was turning in their favour. Setting aside a couple of wild and outrageous claims that 'smuggling had ceased', there was a certain quiet confidence that matters were, or at least might be, improving. Was this sanguine view of the state of smuggling in the Channel justified or was it a matter of 'whistling in the dark'?

In virtually all of the Channel ports there was a small but perceptible increase in the number of seizures during the first decades of the 19th century. Of more import, the erstwhile smuggling strongholds of Barry and Sully Islands had been cleared of smuggling gangs, Flat Holm is not even mentioned in the Customs records of the time and by 1816 even Lundy seemed to be relatively clear of free-traders; indeed much of the island was now given over to farming and its main exports were grain and birds' feathers – thousands of the poor indigenous puffins were culled each year to provide this trade! The Barnstaple Collector reported in 1820 ('with some satisfaction'!) that 'the Island of Lundy is considered to be devoid of smugglers'. For the first time for well over a century there was no longer a smuggling base within the limits of the Bristol Channel.

The establishment of the new preventive stations along the Channel shores, which took place during 1809 to 1812, produced a much stronger numerical presence along the coast. Each station was manned by at least seven men and some of the larger stations by up to twelve. They also provided a regular pattern of patrol along parts of the coasts which hitherto had been sadly lacking any Revenue control. Furthermore, because they are water-borne they were able to provide a swifter and better defence of the numerous isolated bays and coves that were a feature of the coast. The sites of these new preventive stations were, in the main, well selected – Hartland Point, Woolacombe, Combe Martin, Countisbury, Weston-super-Mare and Pill had all figured prominently in the smuggling trade.

Another important factor in the improved detection rate was the more frequent appearance of Revenue vessels in the Channel. The many earnest pleas of various collectors throughout the previous century were, at long last, answered. It is noticeable just how frequently Revenue cutters were involved in seizures at the turn of the century. But not only were more cutters regularly patrolling the Channel waters, but also cutters became based in certain Channel ports, and indeed their very presence had a positive preventive effect on the smuggling trade. The profits to be made from the trade are not so tempting when the risk of capture is higher.

During 1804 to 1806 a small 60 ton cutter, the *Shark*, was stationed at Barnstaple and was then replaced by a much larger vessel, the *Alarm*, which for a period of 15 years alternated between the ports of Barnstaple, Padstow and Ilfracombe. The latter port also had the Excise cutter *Resolution* at various times during the first decades of the century. But the most famous cutter to see service in the Bristol Channel was the *Harpy*. This vessel operated from Ilfracombe during 1823 to 1830; it was a fine sailing cutter of 114 tons, with 18 guns and a crew of 36. It had been built by John Gely of Cowes on the Isle of Wight, who was probably the finest cutter-builder of his time. When the *Harpy* was finally taken out of service in 1837 it was dismasted and towed to a new permanent station on the river Thames near the Tower of London, there to act as a floating station for preventive staff. Up until 1979 there was a floating station berthed off the London Custom House, which was always called the *Harpy*. During the 1830s the *Racer* was based at Bristol and when this vessel departed it was replaced by a small 44 ton cutter, the *Maria*, which spent most of its time at Bridgwater. Besides these vessels the Channel was regularly patrolled by one of the cutters based at Milford Haven and during 1818 to 1822 many Naval vessels seconded to anti-smuggling duties were often seen in the Bristol Channel.

However optimistic the local Customs staff were of some improve-ment in the situation, the Treasury were alive to the dangers which would result from the cessation of the Napoleonic Wars, so much so that they issued a cautionary letter in 1814:

'after so long a period of war in every part of Europe, many of the most daring professional men discharged from their occupation and adverse to the daily labour of agriculture or mechanical employment, will be ready instruments of those desperate persons, who have a little capital and are hardy enough to engage in the trade of smuggling'.

Although elsewhere in England there was plenty of evidence to justify the Treasury's misgivings – some of the most violent and bloody smuggling took place in Kent and Sussex after this time, mainly with the Coast Blockade Service – as far as the Bristol Channel was concerned there were no real signs of any increase of smuggling activity. In fact the Cardiff Collector felt, in 1818, that '[he] had not the least cause to suspect – or believe – that any smuggling is now carried on within the limits of this port.' But as we have already seen the Treasury had placed the Preventive Water-guard under the control of the Admiralty with the strict instructions to make it more 'Naval in organisation'. The whole of the Customs and Excise cutter fleet was also placed with the Admiralty and they came under the control of four Port-Admirals. As far as the west coast was concerned all the cutters were managed from Milford Haven, which had rapidly developed into a Naval port of some consequence.

It is now universally accepted that although the greatest number of men were involved in anti-smuggling duties, there was a woeful lack of co-operation and cohesion between the various forces in-volved – the Waterguard, the Cutter Service, the riding officers and the Customs officers at the ports. Also the cost of these forces had escalated to well over a half a million pounds. The inevitable Parliamentary Committee was formed to examine the problem and it was from its report and recommendations that a 'new' amalga-mated service was formed – the Preventive Waterguard, the cutters and the riding officers (now re-named the Mounted Guard) became the 'Coast Guard' from January 1822, with the control passing back to the Customs Board.

The Bristol Channel area was divided into four Coastguard divisions, which cut across Customs collection boundaries. The first divisional headquarters was at Barnstaple, with 32 men of various ranks to cover the coastline from Bude to Porlock. The Bridgwater division controlled the coast from Porlock to Weston-super-Mare with 24 men. The division centred at Bristol covered the Severn

153

coast as well as across the Channel to Newport with 30 men. Finally the Welsh coast from Cardiff to Llanelly had a complement of 30 men, with its headquarters at Swansea. Thus the Channel was now protected by well over 100 men and at least a couple of Revenue cutters. There had never been such a strong Revenue presence in the Channel.

It would be fitting to be able to report that the Coastguard was an instant success in the Channel, however it was not obvious unless one considers the lack of seizures as a measure of its preventive success. The first Coastguard seizure in the Channel occurred in April 1826 at Shipload Bay – midway between Clovelly and Hartland Point. A detachment of men from the station at Hartland found 20 bales of tobacco, three half-ankers of brandy and ten bottles of wine 'hidden neath the rocks'. The Bay has a steep descent to the shore but it is the only true sandy beach along that stretch of the coast. It did seem a natural spot for smuggling and yet, surprisingly enough, there was no other recorded seizure at the spot.

Just less than one year later the Coastguard and a group of Customs officers from Ilfracombe combined forces to retrieve some 300 ankers of brandy that had been landed on the shore near Heddon's Mouth. Whether they were acting on information is not made clear from the reports. Indeed there had been many problems over seizures made by way of information. It would appear that many officers, both in the Coastguard and the Customs, had not owned up to receiving information; presumably they did not wish to share their seizure rewards with their informants. The Customs Board took a strong view on such matters and they warned all their officers that they were 'liable to suspension' should they not declare the correct circumstances of their seizures and that they were to disclose the full details of their informants.

On this occasion the Revenue men searched the farm buildings belonging to John Hayle, which lay only a short distance from the shore. They discovered no less than 262 ankers of brandy hidden underneath a stable floor, but by this time Hayle had made his escape – through an upstairs bedroom window. In fact he was never captured or convicted of smuggling, and it was the general opinion that 'he had fled the country'. The Customs tried to implicate Hayle's wife for assisting smuggling and harbouring smuggled goods. But after numerous reports to London and much legal debate, the case against her was dropped. Perhaps it was felt that no local jury would convict her. Not much had changed in the intervening years, to obtain a smuggling conviction from prejudiced juries or magistrates had been a constant problem during the previous century.

The Revenue men had to face fierce opposition when they attempted to move their large haul of spirits (worth almost £1,200) to the King's Warehouse. The carriers commissioned for the task were attacked on the road to Ilfracombe, obviously local feelings were running high. It was therefore decided to transport the goods to Barnstaple along a safer route and to where there was a safer warehouse – I suppose fearing a determined effort to rescue the seized cargo. However, it was still felt necessary to await a detachment of militia to guard the consignment en route. This is the only instance in the whole of the Bristol Channel area where there was a direct attempt to recover seized goods; in other parts of the country such rescue operations were quite frequent, even to warehouses being broken into.

Early in 1822 the Coastguard at Bristol were ordered to protect and remove the cargo from the vessel *Fame*, which had wrecked near the mouth of the river Avon. The vessel had been outward bound for Cork and secreted amongst its cargo was a cask which contained '106 instruments of iron apparently well fitted to be fixed to the top of poles, sufficiently long to be managed with effort at a greater distance than a bayonet at the end of a musket'. Not only was the Bristol collector instructed to keep a watch for anyone who might apply for the goods but the Customs Board felt that it was serious enough to inform all the west coast collectors about the discovery, and they were enjoined to watch for 'similar type of arms being exported to Ireland.' Barely 20 years had passed since the French landing in Ireland and the Government was well aware of the possibility of an uprising.

The Gower coast had still not lost its smuggling traditions, despite the fact that it was strongly guarded by the Coastguard. The new force had several small seizures of tobacco and spirits. But in 1829 a party of Coastguardmen found 40 casks of spirits and several boxes of cigars hidden 'under a stack of hay' near Bishopton, which is not very far from Brandy Cove. The goods were thought to have come from a vessel bound for Swansea. At the other end of the Welsh coast, the Customs men from Newport seized 250 kegs of brandy in June 1833 at an empty house near Nash Point. This was very close to the spot Thomas Knight had used in the previous century. The offending vessel was believed to be the *Kate* of Bristol, which had loaded coal for Truro (nowadays it is strange to think of Truro as a port). The Customs men's first suspicions were raised when the

The chase and battle at sea.

vessel only loaded 60 tons 'when it was capable of carrying 100 tons'. The final seizure was directly as a result of information, because two local fishermen witnessed the goods being landed on the shore but they were unable to identify the vessel. The house where the goods were found had been rented by a local publican to a 'stranger', but although a close watch was kept on the house not a soul turned up. Furthermore there was insufficient evidence to connect the *Kate* with the smuggled goods, so the vessel and its master, Henry Davies, were released. The spirits, nearly 1,100 gallons of brandy, were due to be auctioned in Newport until there was a universal protest from the town's publicans that such a large quantity of spirits coming onto the market would ruin their trade! After remaining in the Queen's Warehouse for almost twelve months whilst the debate raged on, the spirits were eventually sent to London for disposal.

One of the early problems experienced by the new service was the quality of the men at their disposal. Despite the fact that the number of seizures increased nationwide, there were many inquiries into the conduct of the men and during 1825 to 1829 no less than 215 were dismissed from the service for various causes – 'drunkenness', 'unsuitable' and 'mutinous and most outrageous conduct' were the most frequent charges. On this subject a rather interesting general order was issued in 1831; 'There being reason to fear that an attempt will be made to corrupt our men through the medium of females; it is directed that patrols hold no communication with any person, either male or female'!

One factor that had a major impact on smuggling in the Bristol Channel was the establishment of the Coastguard in Ireland. For the five years prior to 1820 the amount of tobacco seized in Ireland was less than 10,000 pounds a year, but from the setting-up of the service the seizures increased from some 40,000 pounds to no less than a quarter of a million pounds – a quite staggering figure. Much of the tobacco smuggled into Ireland had ultimately found its way onto the mainland, especially the Welsh and Channel coasts. The success of the new service was such that it forced many American and foreign companies out of the trade, with the result that there were far less goods available for smuggling, which accounted in part for a decrease in the Channel smuggling. Port Rush, which had for many years been a smuggling entrepot, now had a strong Coastguard presence with a staff of one chief officer, nine men and two boats. One Welsh master who regularly traded to Dublin was caused to comment, 'all the fun has gone out of the trade now that the risks are so high. Mark you in the old days I made enough not to bother one way or another'!

The Customs Board had smartened up its ideas on the information front. It had infiltrated informants into the French smuggling ports and from them it received very precise and accurate information on the names and their ports of vessels loading. They also now had their own officers in the Channel Islands. They were also very quick in notifying all their officers (including the Coastguard) of all the special contrivances found hidden on vessels. Indeed the ingenuity of some masters and crew members was quite amazing. In 1836 the Coastguard at Hartland seized the *Tam O'Shanter*, a small smack carrying coals from Cardiff. They found 72 ankers of brandy hidden in the spaces between the cabin and the outer timbers. Just one year later the 72 ton schooner *Good Intent* from Newport was seized off Mounts Bay by the Revenue cutter *Sylvia*. During the search of the vessel the Coastguardmen found 26 ankers in a false lining of the sail locker, 138 ankers were discovered in a space formed by double bulkheads between the forepeak and the hold and finally 21 ankers under the flooring of the forepeak. The bulkheads

157

and the flooring had been newly tarred so that the smell of the spirits should not be too apparent! Full details, with a drawing of concealments, of this seizure was passed to every port and Coastguard station, so the *Good Intent* achieved a certain fame. The master was convicted of smuggling and sentenced to a long term of imprisonment. The vessel was condemned and although the owners (well-known merchants of Newport who maintained that they were not involved in the smuggling) petitioned for its release, the vessel was broken up in 1838 and all the cargo sold at public auction.

Perhaps as a result of this case the Coastguard received a general order,

'. . . to be upon their guard against a common practice amongst vessels returning from a voyage with coals, to any foreign port, of putting Contraband goods on their return into light vessels for landing at the ports but chiefly to Cobles and Fishing Boats at sea . . .'

This order was especially important because in 1831 the coastwise duty on coal had been abolished, so vessels trading coal within the Channel area were no longer under any Revenue control. The export duty on coal survived until 1850.

It is interesting to note that the master of the *Good Intent* received a prison sentence rather than being pressed into the Navy. Compulsory Naval service for convicted smugglers ceased in 1834. Generally impressment into the Navy fell after 1815, but it was never formally abolished. The last Bristol Channel smuggler (as far as I can gather) to be committed to serve in the Navy was William Morgan of the *Prince Regent*, who was convicted of smuggling six pounds of tobacco at Newport in 1830. Morgan was somewhat unlucky, he came ashore at midnight and virtually walked into the arms of a Customs boatman! As a result of this seizure the vessel was re-rummaged and a quantity of brandy and rum was found in the cargo, although the vessel had been already in the port for a number of days.

The Customs officers at Bristol had several notable seizures, not only hidden in compartments but also hidden in cargo, which was otherwise free from duty. Bottles of wine were found concealed in casks of tar, half-bales of tobacco (approximately 65 pounds in weight) cleverly hidden in bales of cotton and even manufactured tobacco made up to look like old ropes and pieces of leather. In 1840 Johan Porter, the mate of the schooner *Elizabeth*, was prosecuted for having '6 periques of tobacco hidden underneath the floor of his cabin', and on the same vessel another quantity of smuggled tobacco was found 'wound up in old sails'. The *Elizabeth* had arrived from

Cork where, according to the Customs report, 'plentiful supplies of contraband tobacco were available'. Porter was sent to prison and rather cheekily he applied to the Customs Commissioners for payment of subsistence whilst he was in Bristol gaol. Amazingly the Customs Board directed the collector to order the governor of the gaol to pay Porter 6d a day on behalf of the City, who were told to call upon the Customs for repayment of the sum! What a change from the old days when smugglers were immured for months upon end without any assistance. The Board later ordered Porter's release from prison after only serving two months of his six months' sentence. Perhaps they felt they had been unwise in granting him any money, as it was becoming rather expensive.

By 1841 when the first Comptroller-General of the Coastguard, Capt. William Bowles, RN, retired, the service had developed into a most efficient and well disciplined organisation largely based on Naval lines and had, indeed, become virtually an adjunct to the Senior Service. Some of the comments by the Bristol Channel collectors reflect this great improvement. At Barnstaple it was considered that 'smuggling has almost been entirely suppressed by the zeal and vigilance of the officers of the Coastguard. Their efforts and their urgency have contributed to a demise of the evil of the trade, which has for so long been a canker on society'! Strong words from a public servant, a body of men more noted for their reserve and guarded comments. The Swansea Collector felt 'the general good-conduct and respectability of the coastguard have contributed greatly to this very desirable state of affairs [the decrease in smuggling]'. However, at Bridgwater the Collector felt that another factor should also be considered, 'the Act of Parliament which makes foreigners liable to the same penalties as Englishmen if caught smuggling has tended more to suppress the traffic than anything that has ever before been done'. I must confess that this statement appears a slight exaggeration. The Act referred to by the Collector was passed in 1834. The problems of foreign smugglers had been quite considerable on the south and east coasts but they were not very remarkable in the Bristol Channel except for the odd Irish smugglers, who rejoiced under such names as 'O'Brien', 'O'Connor' and 'Hennessey' and yet claimed they were of French nationality! But perhaps the Collector was thinking more of the increasing number of foreign crew members who were being caught and convicted of smuggling, largely by concealing the goods on board. As the South Wales ports' foreign traffic rapidly developed so did the number of French, Dutch, Spanish and Cuban names appearing in the smuggling records.

In 1849 the Comptroller-General of the Coastguard, Capt. Houston Stewart, RN gave as his opinion:

'Runs by swift-sailing cutters are seldom now attempted and smuggling where it prevails is generally effected by means of coasting vessels, and vessels entering the ports from foreign countries with contraband goods. These are either secreted under their cargoes or in carefully contrived places of concealment. It is in these cases rather upon the vigilance, activity and intelligence of the officers in the ports rather than upon that of the cruisers or the Coastguard.'

Coming from such an experienced and responsible officer this point of view needs serious consideration as to whether it can be confirmed, at least as far as the Bristol Channel is concerned. Certainly from the records of smuggling over the previous ten years, Capt. Stewart's opinion seems quite valid.

Along the coastline controlled by the Barnstaple division, 108 ankers of brandy had been seized 'near Hartland Point' in 1844, though the smuggling vessel was not captured despite a day-long chase by the Coastguard cutter *Maria*. Just two years later 55 half-bales of tobacco stalks were found on the shore at Ilfracombe but no person convicted. Tobacco stalks were ground down to make snuff, which carried a heavy Excise duty. However, it would appear from the reports that the illegal trade was still going on because 'the insufficiency of the preventive forces' was put forward as the reason for the poor seizure rate.

Further up the coast in the Bridgwater division, the trade appeared to be slightly more active. A fine seizure was made in 1841 at St Audries Bay (near Watchet) when the riding officer (or mounted guard) at Watchet surprised the crew of the sloop *Kitty and Clara* in the actual landing of 124 casks of brandy and geneva. What is even more surprising is that this very intrepid officer not only seized the goods but also managed to seize the vessel. It is not stated just how he achieved this feat but the vessel was finally condemned and destroyed.

In 1843 it was thought that 'many tubs of spirits had been landed in the Weston-super-Mare area', and sure enough during March and April 1843 over 600 ankers of spirits were seized near Sand Bay. We have earlier seen the seizure of spirits near the river Yeo in 1845. Nevertheless it was felt that smuggling was on the decrease, largely attributable to the 'presence and vigilance of the Revenue vessels'. As the *Maria* was stationed at Bridgwater during this period one might say that such a view was rather biased.

The Bristol Collector was very confident in his appraisal of the trade in his division, he considered it 'to be well in hand'. Furthermore he was able to report that due 'to the vigilance and urgency of his dock officers numerous attempts at petty smuggling by crews had been frustrated'. In this context 'petty' seemed to include up to 12 pounds of tobacco and a couple of gallons of spirits. Frequently these petty seizures were made as the crew members went ashore and were probably nothing more than a way to pay for their drinking whilst the crew were in port. Indeed it was suggested in a Report on the Tobacco Trade in 1844 that the crews' wages were deliberately kept low because 'they all have the opportunity to venture in the smuggling trade'.

As far as runs along the coasts were concerned, it was thought that they were very rare, mainly because of the cutter *Racer* which was stationed at Bristol during the 1840s. Certainly the only run of any consequence was '96 casks of brandy seized near Clevedon', the goods came from the coasting vessel *Bridget*, carrying coals from Llanelly. There was a local Court of Inquiry into this seizure because two Coastguardmen were accused of being involved in the landing. They were finally cleared of the charge as the Court found that 'the anonymous letter had been malicious and untrue'.

The Excise was still active in the area. A supervisor seized over 500 pounds of tobacco stalks virtually in the centre of Bristol, on their way to an illicit mill that had been set up in the backyard of a factory. In 1844 an Excise officer seized 57 casks of brandy at North Petherton, just a mile or so inland from Bridgwater. The goods were being moved in an open farm cart in broad daylight!

Over the other side of the Channel, in March 1841, the schooner *Rose* anchored in the mouth of the river Ebbw. The crew had hardly started to discharge the smuggled cargo to waiting farm carts than a party of Newport officers arrived on the scene. They were able to seize 118 casks of brandy, the vessel, the carts and also detain the group of landers – what a coup! The master and mate of the *Rose* were imprisoned, the owners of the vessel (coal merchants of some distinction in the port) received heavy fines despite pleading their innocence and the landers were fined. The owners and the landers were said to have 'river mud on their clothes', which suggested that they had all been involved in the smuggling attempt. The case did little to improve the relations between the Customs at Newport and the merchants because the next few years were marked by a number of accusations levelled at certain officers that they were in collusion with smuggling within the port – all were investigated but none were proved.

161

The romantic view of smuggling – as shown on these cigarette cards first
issued in 1932.

The Swansea division seemed to be rather quiet as far as smuggling was concerned. Although the Collector was prepared to admit that there had been 'frequent attempts to effect landings on the Gower coast and near Nottage, these have not been accomplished because of utmost vigilance of the officers'. However, he did highlight another side to the illegal trade, 'large quantities of cigars are brought by those vessels trading between this port and Cuba with copper ore'. Cigars were very heavily taxed at this time, the rate was 9s 5d per pound, over three times the duty levied on other tobacco goods. It was during this period that Swansea developed rapidly as a major British port with large imports of ore to supply the industries of the Tawe valley.

By 1850, for some unaccountable reason, there was a sudden upsurge of smuggling runs all around the coasts and the Bristol Channel was no exception. In March of that year a French sloop was sighted off the coast near Ilfracombe and the local Coastguard managed to signal the information to a patrolling cutter, the *Asp*, which was based at Milford Haven. The suspect vessel was never caught but two days later ten casks of brandy were washed up on the shore at Minehead. The commander of the *Asp* thought that the vessel in question was the *Georges* of Cherbourg, it and its master Gosselin were well known to the British Customs. The vessel was finally seized in August of the same year near Lyme Regis and Gosselin boasted of the number of successful smuggling runs he had made.

During the last week of May a large schooner, the *Wave*, landed about 8,000 pounds of tobacco stalks at Aberthaw, Portishead and Bridgwater. Although the vessel was not taken, most of the goods were recovered by searches of the shores by the local Coastguard. The *Wave* became a marked vessel and its description was relayed to every port in the United Kingdom, which would make its next entry into the country rather difficult. However, as it was an American owned vessel it probably never came back to the shores, or at least there is no evidence that it did.

In August 1850 a tide-surveyor at Bristol received some information of an intended run on the coast near the mouth of the Avon. By this time the cutter *Racer* had been moved from the port, so with a certain presence of mind the officer impressed a local fishing yawl with the aid of two local fishermen. A French cutter, the *Henri*, the object of his information, was detained near Portishead with over 6,500 pounds of tobacco leaf and stalks on board. The reward for this seizure amounted to £456, of which the tide-surveyor received £228 (over twice his annual salary). The owner of the fishing vessel

163

and the two fishermen were given £9 to share between themselves! The two men who aided in the seizure were quite rightly incensed at the inequality of the treatment and they complained bitterly to their local vicar. He took up their grievance and appealed to the Customs Board on their behalf. After many reports back and forth, the Board ordered the tide-surveyor to pay each man £20 out of his reward. One can be fairly sure that he had minimised their part in the operation.

As the year was coming to a close there was a final flourish across the Channel, when in December 20 ankers of brandy were found hidden near Lavernock Point. Two months later 120 ankers were 'believed to have been run at Penarth'. No goods were found but local information suggested that they had been landed by a French vessel that had come to Cardiff to load coal.

Perhaps it is not surprising to discover that the Comptroller-General is quoted as saying in July 1850:

> 'It is with much regret that I call the attention of the officers and men of the coastguard ashore and afloat to the fact that the contraband trade has greatly increased and that the smugglers appear determined to carry on their illicit practices with increased vigour during the ensuing winter.'

However, with the advantage of hindsight, 1850 appears nothing more than a single unusual year as far as smuggling is concerned, with no apparent reason for the sudden and rather unexpected rise in the trade. The year did not herald a new wave of smuggling and within six years it was considered safe to transfer the Coastguard service away from the Customs department and however much they complained about the change, rightly or wrongly the decision was made. The Coastguard service was now placed under the control of the Admiralty, thus recognising that it had become to all intents and purposes a Royal Naval reserve with wreck and life saving responsibilities, and the protection of the Revenue became almost a minor aspect of its duties. In any case the majority of seizures were now made by the Customs officers at the ports from crew members. As we have already seen just one year after the departure of the Coastguard away from Customs control, the Customs Board were quite sanguine about the smuggling trade.

During the latter years of the 1840s the Customs officers at the ports of Newport, Cardiff and, to a lesser degree, Swansea had to contend with a new smuggling menace – the illegal landings of Irish immigrants. Some years earlier the Collectors of both Newport and Cardiff had reported an influx of 'Irish passengers', though very little official notice was taken of such reports. However, from 1845 onwards, seemingly every vessel arriving from Ireland carried passengers and there were many vessels operating in the Bristol Channel that were solely in the passenger trade, such was the profit to be made out of human suffering. The famine years of 1845 and 1846 had started the exodus and from 1847 – the cholera year in Ireland – the number of immigrants arriving in the Channel ports rose dramatically. The immigrants were drawn to the rapidly expanding coal and iron industries of the Welsh valleys.

The Customs service, among its other many duties, was responsible for the administration and enforcement of the various Passenger Acts that were quickly passed during the period from 1842 to 1855. These Acts were mainly designed to improve the wretched conditions on the emigrant vessels sailing to the Americas, Australia and New Zealand, but nevertheless they applied equally to all vessels carrying passengers, however short the voyage. Under the Acts every vessel was required to be licensed and, according to its size, was restricted to the number of passengers it could legally transport. There were very many instances of unlicensed vessels arriving in the various Channel ports, many without lifeboats and most seemed to flaunt the Acts by carrying an excess number of passengers. Many masters were heavily fined (the going rate appeared to be £5 for each excess person) and those masters who landed passengers without authority, and there were enough of them, received stiff prison sentences.

There were so many instances of illegal landings of passengers at the Welsh ports that it will be sufficient to quote just a couple from the heart-rending list. In May 1847 at Cardiff, the master of the *Catherine* from Clonkelly loaded 25 persons (all women and children) into an open boat at the entrance to the river Taff and from there they had to make their way as best they could. His excuse for this action was, 'fear of getting abused by the inhabitants of the town because the Irish people were in such a diseased and destitute state.' Indeed once they had managed to make it ashore the poor immigrants faced fierce opposition from the local inhabitants, who considered that they brought cholera with them and that the families would ultimately end up on the poor rate. In this instance the master was fined £200 and also given a two months prison sentence.

Two years later the master of the *Mary* from Cork put 20 persons (again women and children) ashore into the mud of the river Ebbw near Newport lighthouse. The other excess passengers were loaded into an open boat, one woman and three children were drowned when the boat capsized. This master was fined £150 and sent to gaol   165 for three months but there was no hint of a manslaughter charge being brought against him. There were also several examples of immigrants being landed on deserted beaches well away from the large towns and ports.

Such a trade was nigh on impossible to control, often the wretched passengers were concealed in the cargo holds or the bilges in the vain hope of avoiding discovery and the conditions in which they travelled were deplorable. The number of prosecutions only underline the extent of the trade. However, by 1855, most of the large scale immigration had ceased and this despicable trade in human cargo was a thankfully short but nevertheless shameful episode in the Bristol Channel smuggling story.

In its review of smuggling in 1862 the Customs Board reported:

'It must be remembered that in the two principal articles which are subject to the illegal trade, namely tobacco and spirits, there has been no reduction of duty on the contrary the duty on spirits has considerably increased. . . . Furthermore the freeing of duty from many articles has had the effect of diminishing smuggling in detail; we are speaking of smuggling which takes place on the coast, which the Coastguard are appointed to prevent. There was and always will be a great deal of smuggling on board ships and in the harbour and docks.'

To counter such smuggling the Customs Board had reorganised its preventive forces. There were now preventive officers and men stationed at Barnstaple, Ilfracombe (no longer a collection in its own right), Bideford, Appledore, Bridgwater, Minehead, Watchet, Uphill, Bristol, Newport, Cardiff, Aberthaw, Barry, Sully, Swansea, Newton Oxwich, Aberavon and Neath. Though, in truth, there is little evidence of much smuggling other than in the main three Welsh ports and Bristol. It is interesting to note that during 1858 and 1859 the smuggling of brandy virtually ceased, largely due to the failure in two successive years of the French vine crop. And yet by the mid 1860s there was a sudden increase in the smuggling of brandy. The explanation (at least according to the Customs Board) for this upsurge was a general outbreak of cholera in the country; brandy was considered to have valuable prophylactic properties in countering the dreaded disease.

However, without a question of a doubt the most smuggled commodity during the next 75 years would be tobacco. The prevention of tobacco smuggling became the all abiding preoccupation of the preventive officers at the ports. During the 1870s the incidence of tobacco smuggling appeared to be on the increase, judging by the number of seizures made, some of which were quite large. Other than the odd 'old fashioned' run on the south coast all the seizures were made from crew members. It was reported in 1875 that 'the temptation to smuggle offered by the high duties on tobacco must always induce attempts to defraud this Revenue'. Most ports were fairly successful in finding smuggled tobacco and cigars, although it was considered that 'the general use of steam has greatly increased the difficulties of the rummaging officers, spaces in connection with machinery, which can only be searched when they have become cool, are becoming favorite places of concealment.' (The numbers of engine-room men who were convicted for smuggling offences greatly reinforced this opinion.)

A battle between the smugglers and the military.

The officers in the major Channel ports all had notable successes. The suspect vessels were those arriving from certain North European ports (notably Hamburg) and North America; it was in these places that tobacco could be obtained at a very cheap rate. In 1871, at Bristol, the *Horsa* arrived from Hamburg with timber. After a long and careful search, over 250 pounds of tobacco and 21 pounds of cigars were found in the coal bunkers. The whole crew was liable to detention and prosecution as well as the vessel being liable to seizure. However, one crew member owned up to responsibility for the goods and he was heavily fined. It became normal practice for 167 one crew member in turn to admit ownership of the smuggled goods in the event of their discovery and no doubt the resultant fine was shared by all the crew. Certainly on foreign vessels this practice became an almost unwritten law of the sea. As to the seizure of the vessel this depended on whether it was felt that insufficient control or negligence had been shown by the master and the ships' officers. It was considered that as 'responsible' officers, they should not condone smuggling. However, many masters and mates not only overlooked smuggling but actually were involved themselves.

In the same year a British vessel, the *Malta*, arrived at Cardiff to load a cargo of coal. The vessel was searched on arrival but no smuggled goods were found. However, three days later a donkey-man (he worked in the engine room stoking the boilers) was stopped in the dock area with a quantity of tobacco carefully wrapped in a parcel. As a consequence the vessel was re-rummaged and this time 462 pounds of manufactured tobacco and cigars were found in a hollow beam in the engine room. The concealment was so cleverly devised that details of the seizure were circulated to every port. Just a few years later a French vessel, the *La Bayonne*, came with a cargo of timber to Bridgwater. It had been in the port for over a week when a local policeman stopped a drunken crew member near the quay. The man boasted of how he brought in tobacco to pay for his drinking whilst he was ashore. The vessel was thoroughly rumm-aged and nearly 150 pounds of tobacco and cigars were discovered packed in small individual packets. The packages were hidden all over the vessel, in the engine room, the paint lockers, the forepeak and the coal bunkers. Considering the vessel was a regular trader to the port, the Collector had to admit that the trade had been going on for some time without discovery, so much so that the crew had their own ready contacts within the town.

There were many, many seizures of tobacco in the main Channel ports over the next 30 years, but most of them were of minor significance, justifying the Customs Board's opinion that 'attempts at smuggling have been of a petty description and unusually rare during the last year [1870] and very few seizures of importance have been made'. Nevertheless tobacco smuggling did increase steadily until its peak year of 1882, when over 1,500 persons were convicted of smuggling some 25,000 pounds of tobacco – really a flea bite compared with the figures of a century earlier. (In 1789 over 400,000 pounds of tobacco had been seized.) The duty on tobacco was an immense revenue earner for the country, not only did it account for almost 45% of the total Customs duties but it was only slightly less than the total yield for income tax (this was the good old days when income tax was just 6d in the £1!). The duty on tobacco stood at 3s 6d per pound, which was equivalent to over 400% by value. As virtually 90% of the tobacco was sold in half-ounces to the poorer and working classes, there was a large and ready market for any cheap tobacco. It is interesting to note that not until the 1880s did cigarettes begin to be made in this country, indeed most of the famous brands, Woodbine, Players and Gold Flake date from this time. It is reputed that the habit of cigarette smoking was picked up by the soldiers serving in the Crimean War, but there is no evidence of any cigarette smuggling until the turn of the century. However, 1882 proved to be a watershed and from that year the smuggling figures steadily declined. For the first time for almost 200 years smuggling became a rather minor problem for the Customs authorities.

In 1882 there was one seizure in the Bristol Channel which is worthy of note. In June of that year a Spanish vessel, the *San Tamo*, arrived from Bilbao with a cargo of pit-props. Almost ten days after its arrival the Customs made a surprise rummage and found 572 pounds of tobacco hidden in the remaining cargo. The pit-props had been cleverly arranged to form a large and deep cavity in the cargo capable of holding far more goods than were found. The vessel was seized on the premise that the ships' officers must have had foreknowledge of such an elaborate concealment. The legality of the seizure of the vessel was argued at length and after the urgent intervention of the local Spanish Consul the Customs Board agreed to release the vessel, but both the master and the chief mate were heavily fined. The Collector was obviously delighted with the seizure and he ended one of his reports by saying, 'the crews of these vessels are only deterred from becoming regular smugglers on a small scale on each voyage by the increasing vigilance of our rummaging officers'. In this instance I have the feeling that the local Customs staff must have received some information to suggest that there were smuggled goods on board.

Since the Coastguard had been taken over by the Admiralty the number of stations and men had been drastically reduced. By 1906 the Customs Board felt it time for this policy of retrenchment to be seriously questioned:

'As such extensive reductions would appear to indicate that the Lords of the Admiralty have definitely decided to abolish all Coastguard stations which are not required for strictly Naval purposes. We would point out the serious bearing upon the safety of the Customs revenue. . . . However, the paucity of detections by the Coastguard of smuggling is not evidence that a coast guard is not necessary. All inlets, creeks and shores, which

169

are accessible to boats should be regarded as possible centres of smuggling and some system of guard and watch should be maintained.'

The Customs Board were seeking sole responsibility for protecting the Revenue along all the coasts of the United Kingdom.

As far as the Bristol Channel was concerned there had not been a great deal of reduction either in stations or manpower, not because of the smuggling possibilities but rather acknowledging the dangerous nature of the coasts – the main Coastguard duties were now concerned with wreck and life saving. There were still stations at Appledore, Lundy Island, Ilfracombe, Lynmouth, Minehead, Watchet, Penarth, Nells Point (Barry), Lantwit, Porthcawl, Mumbles, Oxwich and Rhossili. The inevitable reorganization of the Coastguard service was delayed until after the First World War and in April 1923 its control was passed to the Board of Trade. The Customs and Excise Board (the two services had been amalgamated in 1909) took over the whole control of smuggling. They set up a new force called the Land Preventive service, which acted as a supplement to the existing Waterguard officers. Each Coast Preventive man had a stretch of coast to regularly patrol to report movements of ships – a latter day riding officer on a motor cycle rather than a horse! Nothing much changes!

In 1914 there was an unusual and rather exciting incident in the Bristol Channel. For almost three years before the outbreak of war the Customs and Excise Board had been represented on a committee which had been set up to determine what action would be necessary at the ports if war was declared. Sealed copies of instructions were deposited with all collectors, which were only to be opened on receipt of a certain codeword. By the end of July, when war seemed imminent, the codeword was sent out, and the collectors were aware of the action required and were able to plan accordingly.

Within an hour of the Board receiving a telegram from the Foreign Office (at 11.17 pm on 4th August 1914) all collectors had received the further codeword for action. The first priority was the seizure of every German merchant vessel in the ports. All these vessels would be detained for the duration of the war, and their cargo was treated as 'enemy cargo'. As a result of this action two vessels were seized in Bristol, one in both Cardiff and Swansea. The Chairman of the Board was able to report, 'By seven o'clock every German vessel in the United Kingdom was safely tied up.'

It was a different matter for vessels seized at sea. They were condemned as prizes of war, a memory of the days of Nelson. The only vessel that was seized at sea by the Customs was a large

German merchant vessel called the *Belgia*. This vessel was anchored near the English and Welsh Lightship in the Bristol Channel awaiting a berth in Newport Docks. The Newport collector felt that this ship would escape unless he took some steps to arrest it. He requisitioned the Dock Company's tug, and along with several officers boarded the *Belgia* about seven miles from the port and formally arrested the vessel. It was brought into Newport, the wireless dismantled and guards placed on board. The collector's prompt, if somewhat unusual, action caused some embarrassment at first, although later he was praised for his efforts. He subsequently applied to the Prize Court at the Admiralty for a share of the prize money, the vessel having been valued at £750,000. However, he was informed that a reward was not applicable in this case. It is interesting to note that he had been on duty continuously for over 37 hours, which resulted in a breakdown of his health and he was away on sick leave for over two months. Such is the reward for such a bold and enterprising operation!

Perhaps one of the most unusual smuggling cases of the inter-war years occurred in the Bristol Channel – the smuggling of greyhounds from Eire! The greyhounds – each valued at £60 to £70 (when the weekly wage was £2) – were bought in Cork, transported across Eire, smuggled over the Land Boundary and finally taken on a coastal collier at Belfast. The dogs were brought to Penarth Docks and as the vessel was purely in the coasting trade, it received scant interest from the Customs staff. The greyhounds were carried off the vessel late at night and delivered to the greyhound tracks in Cardiff and Merthyr Tydfil. The local Customs officer received some information about the trade, and on the vessel's next arrival in the port it was thoroughly searched. Three greyhounds were found in the forepeak. The master admitted that he had smuggled nearly 60 dogs during the previous 18 months – a rather profitable trade by any standard. With the Customs duty then standing at 40%, it was reckoned he had defrauded the Revenue out of nearly £1,500. Which only goes to prove that if there is a sufficient profit element any goods will be smuggled.

The conditions at the end of the Second World War were ideal for a resurgence of smuggling. High tariffs, punitive rates of Purchase Tax, rationing and a general scarcity of goods were all incentives for the very profitable illegal trade. Apart from the regular smuggled goods, such as cigarettes, cigars, tobacco and spirits, anything that was in short supply was meat and drink for the smuggler. The list seemed to be endless – tinned foodstuffs, butter, cosmetics, razor blades, records, fountain pens, lighters, cameras, watches, jewellery, 171 chocolate, saccharin . . . but the item which appeared to be the favourite, and the smuggling of which became a post-war phenomenon, was nylon stockings. The fibre had not been introduced until 1939, and nylons were virtually unobtainable in this country. They cost around 7s to 8s in America and could be sold in this country for around £1, and they were also relatively easy to conceal. Virtually every vessel that came from America carried large quantities of smuggled nylons. It was reported that a firm in New York supplied large quantities to British crews on credit terms.

As British trade increased in the post-war years, the Channel ports experienced a boom with vessels queueing up for berths at Avonmouth, Bristol, Cardiff, Newport and Swansea. The Bristol Channel was one of the busiest waterways around the coast and because of its situation there was a flourishing trade with the United States of America; this trade brought in its wake an upsurge in smuggling. The number of seizures of nylons and the inevitable American cigarettes was quite colossal during the fifties and early sixties. This writer started his Customs career in the South Wales ports during this period and every newly arrived vessel that was rummaged seemed to yield smuggled goods, many of a considerable size.

Each different nationality appeared to have their own favourite places of concealment. The omnipresent Dutch coasters that plied the various Channel ports, both large and small, were known as inveterate smugglers and furthermore recognised as the most resourceful. They generally favoured clever concealments in the engine room – though their geneva or Dutch gin never gained true popular appeal. The Spanish vessels which brought iron ore, pit props and citrus fruits, frequently had goods hidden in the cargo and the cheap Spanish brandy found a ready market in all Channel ports. The German crews specialised in hidden compartments in the cabins or saloons, whereas the Swedes and Norwegians preferred to conceal their goods in the cargo holds and deck stores where they could keep a watchful eye whilst they worked on deck. Those years were indeed a bonanza time for the smugglers. The steady reduction of duties and rates of purchase tax and the cessation of rationing slowly brought this smuggling boom to a close.

Nowadays the situation is vastly different. In 1987–8 the Customs and Excise department seized 163 tons of tobacco, almost eight million cigarettes, one quarter of a million cigars and some 44,000 litres of alcoholic drinks – so the old bastions of the smuggling trade still survive. However, the major smuggling problem facing the Customs and Excise is the illegal importation of drugs – mainly cannabis, heroin and cocaine. In 1988 the number and size of drug seizures was up by 60% on the previous year and the total 'street value' of all drugs seized was £185 million. Cocaine and heroin remain the major threat to the United Kingdom as more and more drugs (especially cocaine) are targeted by the smugglers on this country. Though much of the drug smuggling, and indeed other smuggling, is confined to the ports and airports, small craft carrying cannabis have used deserted bays and creeks to land their cargoes. Indeed the view expressed by the Customs Board back in 1906 is equally valid today – 'all inlets, creeks and shores, which are accessible to boat should be regarded as possible centres of smuggling'.

As if to emphasise that no port or stretch of coast is safe from the drug smugglers, in December 1988 a large quantity of cocaine was found on the *Mediteran Frigo* at Newport. Seven kilogrammes of the drug with a street value of £2 million was a most significant seizure. The vessel, bound from Colombia (one of the major countries producing the narcotic drug) to Belgium, was loaded with bananas. It was shadowed up the Bristol Channel by one of the fast Customs cutters, to ensure that none of the drugs were off-loaded in the Channel.

Thus the story of smuggling in the Bristol Channel has come full circle. It is a long, long way from the days of Knight, Arthur, Robinson et al and albeit that the story to be told has been less exciting than the tales of smuggling around the other coasts of Britain, it has been thankfully less violent and bloody. I hope what it has shown is that this unique and important waterway has an individuality and romance all of its own, which has been reflected in its smuggling ways, as befits the Severn Sea which 'shines as bright As any moon on trucks of coal'.

GLOSSARY

Anker: A measure of spirits, roughly 7½ gallons; half anker 3½ to 4 gallons.

Bat: A long wooden stave used as a weapon by smugglers.

Boatsitter: A chief boatsman in the Preventive Waterguard.

Coast Blockade: The preventive system in Kent and Sussex, 1817–31.

Coastguard: (first called the Coast Guard) The national preventive service established under Capt W Bowles, appointed 1822.

Coastwaiter: The Customs officer responsible for vessels from home ports.

Collector: The head of the customs personnel at each port.

Comptroller: The Collector's deputy at the larger ports.

Cutter: A single-masted vessel, rigged like a sloop but with a running bowsprit.

Dragoon: A mounted soldier.

Exciseman: An officer responsible for assessing and collecting Excise Duty.

Flink Pistol: Used to flash a signal; in appearance like a starting gun.

Free trader: A smuggler.

Galley: A large open rowboat, typically propelled by up to 20 oars.

Gauger: An Exciseman responsible for measuring spirits and calculating duty.

Geneva: Gin, also known as Hollands.

Hanger: A sword.

Jacobite: A supporter of James II after his abdication, or of his son.

Landwaiter: The Customs Official who supervised the unloading of ships from foreign ports.

Lugger: A vessel with four-cornered sails, rigged fore-and-aft.

Militia: A military unit, sometimes a volunteer unit. Mainly established under Acts of 1757–8, when men were chosen to serve by ballot, but substitutes were allowed.

Owler: Anyone smuggling wool out of England.

Preventive Waterguard: Preventive service established in 1809 covering whole country in 3 districts; patrols by cutters and small preventive boats.

Privateer: A privately-owned armed vessel holding a government commission (Letters of Marque) to wage war on enemy ships.

Riding Officer: Officer in the Customs service appointed to patrol on horse-back, initially to counter the owling trade.

Run: A successful landing of contraband.

Safe House: An inn or other building providing a recognised refuge for smugglers, usually with storage and stabling.

Sloop: or Shallop. A small single-masted, fore-and-aft rigged ship.

Sowing a crop: Sinking a raft of tubs in a marked position offshore.

Spout lantern: A signalling lantern made to send out a beam of light through a long spout attachment.

Tap: An unlicenced beer house.

Tide surveyor: The Customs officer responsible for rummaging (searching) vessels anchored in port.

Tub: A wooden cask holding a ½ anker of spirits (3½–4 gallons); often roped in pairs to be carried over the shoulder.

Whig: (originally) A member of the political party which supported the revolution of 1688; the party led by Sir Robert Walpole.

Index